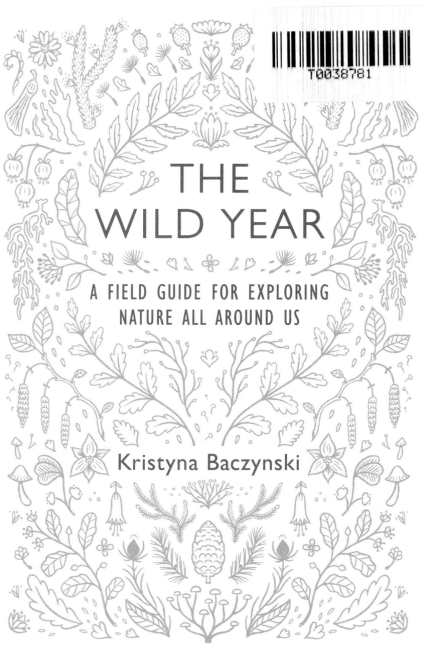

THE
WILD YEAR

A FIELD GUIDE FOR EXPLORING
NATURE ALL AROUND US

Kristyna Baczynski

A TarcherPerigee Book

tarcherperigee

an imprint of Penguin Random House LLC
penguinrandomhouse.com

Most TarcherPerigee books are available at special quantity discounts for bulk purchase for sales promotions, premiums, fund-raising, and educational needs. Special books or book excerpts also can be created to fit specific needs. For details, write: SpecialMarkets@penguinrandomhouse.com.

Library of Congress Cataloging-in-Publication Data

Names: Baczynski, Kristyna, 1986– author.
Title: The wild year: a field guide for exploring nature all around us / Kristyna Baczynski.
Other titles: Field guide for exploring nature all around us
Description: First edition. | [New York]: TarcherPerigee, Penguin Random House LLC, [2022]
Identifiers: LCCN 2022007189 (print) | LCCN 2022007190 (ebook) |
ISBN 9780593538364 (trade paperback) | ISBN 9780593538371 (epub)
Subjects: LCSH: Wild flowers—Pictorial works. | Plants—Pictorial works. |
Nature—Pictorial works. | Field guides.
Classification: LCC QK98.B23 2022 (print) | LCC QK98 (ebook) |
DDC 582.13—dc23/eng/20220304
LC record available at https://lccn.loc.gov/2022007189
LC ebook record available at https://lccn.loc.gov/2022007190

Printed in the United States of America
1st Printing

INTRODUCTION

This book began six years ago, during a cold, dark winter in the North of England. I was sitting in my home studio—a spare room in an apartment that lacked any outdoor space—weary between freelance projects and gripped with seasonal gloom. I started taking walks around my neighborhood to shake up my motivation and noticed little plants thriving despite the frosty bleakness. What were these intrepid leaves? How could they prosper when everything else seemed to have faded? Those brave weeds reignited my curiosity and enthusiasm; I wanted to explore and discover, to document and research, to write and illustrate. That winter I self-published a pocket-size zine that collected together my favorite plants and their fascinating histories. Eventually I made a zine for every season, and together those pages became an early version of *The Wild Year*.

I hope this book can help you connect with the wild plants growing around you, whether you're on an epic hiking adventure or a casual neighborhood stroll.

FORAGING NOTES

Foraging can be an amazing way to enjoy seasonal plants and experiment with new ingredients. However, it can also be dangerous, as misidentification may lead to interaction with irritants and ingestion of toxic matter.

It's always worth foraging with someone who is experienced, knowledgeable, and confident in identifying local plants. It's also advantageous to wear protective gloves and take containers to collect cuttings.

Every plant in this book is accompanied by its scientific name. This is to avoid misidentification, as some plants have look-alikes or share common names across different regions and cultures. For example, in North America *groundnut* refers to a leguminous vine that produces subterranean edible tubers (*Apios americana*, page 130), whereas in South America *groundnut* refers to the herbaceous peanut plant (*Arachis hypogaea*), and in West Africa you would find yet another plant with edible underground pods called *groundnut* (*Vigna subterranea*).

The many types of groundnut, left to right: Apios americana, vigna subterranea, and arachis hypogaea.

You can use the official plant classifications to assist in accurately cross-referencing images and descriptions for more confident identification.

All the plants in this book are broadly categorized by season, based on when each plant is at its peak, most striking, or most useful. These are intended as a guide, as some plants may appear out of season, depending on regional habitat and local climate. You can use the Field Notes section at the back of this book to add more specific details and clarifications as you discover the plants around you.

If you're at all unsure about a plant, do not touch or eat it. Take a photo, make a note, and keep exploring.

❄ CHECKLIST ❄

- ☐ American wintergreen
- ☐ Hairy bittercress
- ☐ Douglas fir
- ☐ Honesty
- ☐ Wolf lichen
- ☐ Common chickweed
- ☐ English ivy
- ☐ Staghorn sumac
- ☐ Candlesnuff fungus
- ☐ Mistletoe
- ☐ European yew
- ☐ Houseleek
- ☐ Red osier dogwood
- ☐ Turkey tail
- ☐ Maidenhair spleenwort
- ☐ Yellow brain
- ☐ Cherry laurel
- ☐ Common gorse
- ☐ Oakmoss lichen
- ☐ Shepherd's purse

WINTER

AMERICAN WINTERGREEN

GAULTHERIA PROCUMBENS

This hardy evergreen is native to North America and can be found in the northeastern United States and Canada. It grows in shrubby clumps up to 6 inches high, preferring shady, forested areas and cool temperatures.

It has glossy, deep green leaves that grow all year and can take on a purple blush in colder months. In summer it produces small, waxy, bell-shaped flowers, which can be white or sometimes pale pink.

These are followed by long-lasting, bright-red berries with pale, mealy flesh that persist from autumn into winter.

Both the leaves and berries are highly aromatic, with a medicinal, minty scent. As the leaves can be foraged, crushed, and fermented to make a refreshing tea, the plant is sometimes called teaberry, which became a common flavor for candies, ice creams, and chewing gum in the early twentieth century.

TEABERRY

TEABERRY

Wintergreen also has many traditional and medicinal uses. A fragrant essential oil can be extracted from its leaves and used, once safely diluted, as a balm to ease congestion, or a topical rub for relieving sore muscles and rheumatism. The plant contains methyl salicylate, a chemical closely related to aspirin, which lends it these pain-fighting properties. However, people who are allergic to aspirin are often also allergic to wintergreen.

WINTERGREEN

ASPIRIN

Other species and varieties of *Gaultheria* exist, varying in size and color, but *G. procumbens* is the most common in North America.

HAIRY BITTERCRESS

CARDAMINE HIRSUTA

This small, flowering weed is native to Europe but has naturalized throughout most of the world, including North America. It can be found peeking out of pavement cracks, wall crevices, and disturbed soils. It prefers cooler temperatures and moist conditions, dying back completely in hot weather.

In late winter its green leaves are among the first foliage to appear, growing in low rosettes up to 8 inches across. The radiating lower stems, which are sometimes blushed with a purple hue, hold rows of round or kidney-shaped leaflets that increase in size as they grow outward. Despite its common name, the plant isn't actually that hairy, with only a few long hairs at the base of each stem. A central flowering stalk shoots up to 10 inches high, tipped with a cluster of tiny, delicate white blooms.

The flowers are followed by rod-shaped seedpods in spring, which measure up to an inch long. They look like miniature green beans and remain on the plant after the flowers and leaves die back, turning reddish brown as they mature. The pods explode when touched, flinging seeds several feet from the original plant, ready to settle and germinate in new nooks and crannies. This kinetic dispersal gives the plant some great alternative common names:

Shot weed, flick weed, and splitting Jenny

Revenge is a dish best served cold.

Hairy bittercress is considered a spreading, nuisance weed by many gardeners. However, the lower leaves are edible and can be foraged as pretty microgreens. Best eaten raw, they have a high vitamin C content and a cress-like flavor, perfect for salads, sandwiches, and garnishes. So put away the weed killer: don't get angry—get hungry!

DOUGLAS FIR

PSEUDOTSUGA MENZIESII

This evergreen tree is a North American native and grows on straight trunks that can span 5 feet in diameter and easily reach over 70 feet high. It is found in forested, mountainous, and rainy areas of North America and in western parts of Europe and the United Kingdom, where it was introduced by Scottish botanist David Douglas, for whom it was named.

The female cones of this tree are pendulous and scaled. Above each scale protrudes a bract, which has a distinctive three-pointed shape that looks like the back half of a mouse disappearing inside. This has led to myths about mice escaping forest fires and seeking refuge in the cones of the Douglas fir. There is a grain of truth to this, as the highly ridged mature bark is corky and moist, which makes it fire resistant.

The bright-green, vitamin-rich young needles can be used to make a tea that has a tangy and rich citrus flavor. Older or dried needles can be used as a rosemary-like herb in savory stews or added to cookies. Spring buds are often used as a flavoring in liqueurs and schnapps.

HONESTY

LUNARIA ANNUA

This wildflower is native to the Balkans and southwest Asia but has naturalized throughout many temperate regions of the world, where it grows along paths, in hedgerows, and on waste grounds. Honesty has a long, upright stalk with toothy, heart-shaped leaves and reaches 20 to 35 inches tall. In spring and summer it is topped with purple or white flowers.

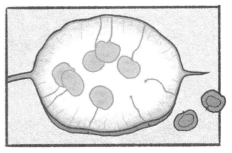

By winter, the pretty blooms of honesty have withered away, but its papery, silver seedpods remain.

The *Lunaria* part of its scientific name refers to these iconic, moon-shaped discs.

In Denmark it is known as *judaspenge*, meaning the "coins of Judas." One person's honesty is another person's biblical betrayal.

WOLF LICHEN

LETHARIA VULPINA

This bright, shrubby lichen can be found on exposed branches and areas of broken bark on both living and dead trees. It appears most often in the coniferous forests of western North America and western Europe, in single or clustered clumps that can individually reach 3 inches in diameter. Wolf lichen is highly tolerant of cool temperatures and grows throughout the winter.

Densely branched with a highly textured, coral-like vegetative surface, wolf lichen is a vivid lime green, which is due not to chlorophyll but vulpinic acid—a chemical poisonous to most mammals, making this a rare toxic lichen.

ACID

Even in winter, when food is scarce, deer, bears, and sheep alike do not graze upon it and leave it undisturbed.

Lichen is off the menu.

What a thoughtful gift!

Wolf lichen has a history of use by humans for controlling wolf and fox populations. Some Scandinavian hunters gathered it to hide in meat that was left in forests for unwanted predators to ingest.

In North America, some Indigenous nations soaked arrowheads in a solution containing this lichen to make them poisonous.

COMMON CHICKWEED

STELLARIA MEDIA

Chickweed may be one of the most common flowering weeds on the planet. It is a European native but widely naturalized across North America, where it can be found almost anywhere, from open lawns and forest edges to empty lots and footpaths. It prefers cool but not freezing weather and flowers from midwinter onward, though it can be found at any time of year in milder regions. It grows in verdant, ground-covering mats that rarely reach more than a few inches in height but readily spread outward.

Chickweed's stems are straggly, flimsy, and rounded with a single row of tiny hairs on one side, which is helpful for identification.

The leaves are oval and opposite, varying in size from ¼ inch to 1½ inches. The white flowers are even smaller, only ¼ inch across when open, with five petals that are deeply divided to give the illusion of ten. This shape lends the plant its official *Stellaria* name, which means "starlike" in Latin.

As its common name suggests, the plant is a much-loved snack for grazing chickens and poultry, as well as other wild animals. Don't let the nibbly birds have all the fun, though; the leaves and stems can be foraged and used raw as an addition to salads and sandwiches, or as a pretty garnish for soups.

Another unusual feature of chickweed is that both its flowers and leaves react to sunlight, opening in the day and closing at night. Larger leaves will fold against the stem at night to protect young shoots.

ENGLISH IVY
HEDERA HELIX

This climbing evergreen vine readily covers trees, walls, and fences in wild areas and gardens. It is native to Europe and western Asia but has naturalized in North America, where it can be invasive.

English ivy can reach over 80 feet high when growing on suitably tall structures, but it may also grow as matted ground cover in open areas. It produces shiny, veined leaves all year round, which appear in two shapes: a three- to five-pointed leaf on young climbing stems and a simpler oval leaf on mature flowering stems.

Zzzz.

This dense tangle of foliage provides safe winter shelter for roosting birds, bats, and hibernating animals.

English ivy blooms in autumn, with a circular spray of small flowers arranged on an umbel dome. These mature into black berries by winter. Both flowers and berries offer a precious late food source for pollinators such as moths and birds.

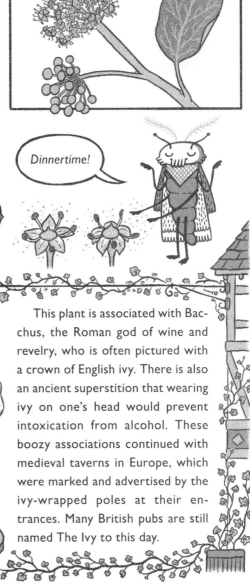

Dinnertime!

This plant is associated with Bacchus, the Roman god of wine and revelry, who is often pictured with a crown of English ivy. There is also an ancient superstition that wearing ivy on one's head would prevent intoxication from alcohol. These boozy associations continued with medieval taverns in Europe, which were marked and advertised by the ivy-wrapped poles at their entrances. Many British pubs are still named The Ivy to this day.

STAGHORN SUMAC

RHUS TYPHINA

This shrubby tree is native to eastern North America and grows 5 to 15 feet high, with a broad spray of branches. In the wild it flourishes in well-draining, rocky soils along sunny borders and open areas. It has been cultivated for its ornamental beauty and now has a much wider range, including Europe.

Staghorn sumac is of visual interest in every season: In spring its arching branches become covered in deep green, spear-shaped leaves that are finely serrated and neatly paired along their stems. In early summer vivid green flowers appear in upright cones that measure 4 to 8 inches high.

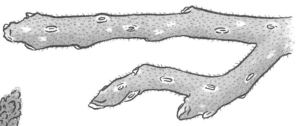

By autumn the flowering cones are pollinated, maturing into upturned, fuzzy, red fruit cones, and the plant's foliage turns shades of orange and crimson.

However, it is the winter display that gives this plant its name, as the leaves shed to reveal the bare maroon stems, velvety and branched like antlers. The fruit cones also remain on female trees, deep burgundy torches that smolder in the wintry darkness.

Staghorn sumac fruits are called bobs and are edible, with a tangy, acidic taste. The fuzz-covered berries can be harvested in autumn and winter—depending on the region and rainfall—and used fresh to make wild lemonade, or dried and crushed to make a colorful, lemony spice. The plant is called vinegar tree in some European countries because of its sharp flavor.

CANDLESNUFF FUNGUS

XYLARIA HYPOXYLON

This spooky little fungus can appear throughout the year, growing on decaying forest floors across Europe and North America.

Candlesnuff grows most abundantly in late autumn, when wispy black spikes emerge on rotting wood. By winter, they can reach 1 or 2 inches tall, with black or gray bases and powdery-white, spore-laden tips, which make them more noticeable and easy to identify. Their common name originates from this display, as they resemble the ashy remnants of burned-out candlewicks.

By spring, the mature fungus becomes more branched and can lose its white coating, leaving twisted black scraps that look like a bundle of spent matches—or, as another common name describes them:

Carbon antlers

Remarkably, this fungus contains trace amounts of phosphorus in its mycelium, which has bioluminescent properties. The amounts are so small it would be difficult to observe this phenomenon in the wild, but when using a long exposure camera in controlled conditions, the ends of these little candlewicks do actually glow.

MISTLETOE
VISCUM ALBUM

This evergreen plant can be found hanging from the branches of trees and shrubs, especially hawthorn, apple, and poplar. It is native to Europe and western Asia but cultivated in many regions of the Northern Hemisphere as a decoration for winter celebrations.

Quite the romantic parasite!

Mistletoe is easiest to find in winter, when surrounding foliage has fallen away to reveal its evergreen leaves and white berries. The plant grows in a clump that measures 1 to 3 feet in diameter and hangs from a host tree. Once it has taken root, it steals its host's water and nutrients to grow.

The modern tradition of hanging mistletoe and kissing under it can be traced back to many ancient cultures. In Rome and Greece it was a symbol of fertility and romance, hung during winter solstice festivities, or smooched beneath as a good-luck charm during wedding celebrations.

Well, hello . . .

EUROPEAN YEW

TAXUS BACCATA

This broad evergreen tree is native to Europe, northern Africa, and western Asia. It has dense branches that grow from a thick trunk with scaly bark. Yew trees can reach 30 to 60 feet high depending on age. Some trees live for centuries, with a number of British specimens exceeding a thousand years of age.

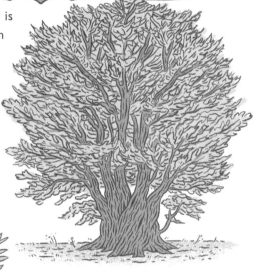

The narrow, needlelike leaves are leathery and bright green. In autumn and winter, seeds, which are covered in a red, berrylike sheath and measure half an inch across, appear on the end of its branches. The bark, leaves, and seeds are all highly toxic and poisonous to humans and animals.

As yew trees age, the older heartwood is often rotted away by a fungus, while the outer layers stay healthy. In some trees this creates a hollow space within the base of the trunk, which can look like a gnarly woodland doorway or an enclosed hideaway.

Yew trees have a rich folkloric history and are regarded as a symbol of life and death, rebirth and renewal, because old branches that seem dead may droop and touch the ground, taking root and forming new trees.

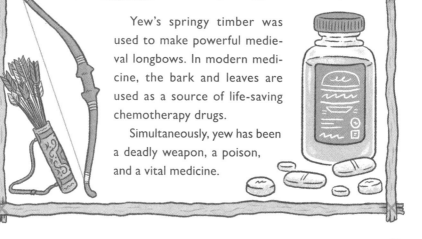

Yew's springy timber was used to make powerful medieval longbows. In modern medicine, the bark and leaves are used as a source of life-saving chemotherapy drugs.

Simultaneously, yew has been a deadly weapon, a poison, and a vital medicine.

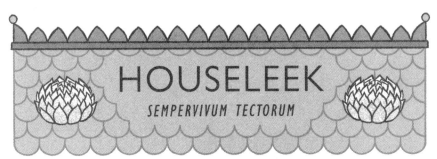

HOUSELEEK
SEMPERVIVUM TECTORUM

This succulent plant is native to the mountainous regions of southern Europe, but is cultivated widely throughout Europe and beyond. It grows in sandy, gravelly soils; enjoys full sunshine; and can often be found growing on rooftops and in rockeries.

Houseleeks grow in evergreen rosettes that measure 4 inches across, consisting of fleshy, pointed leaves that are green and often tipped with purple. Multiple plants often appear together, with a central "mother" rosette sending out spreading stems that generate smaller plants, which is why houseleek is sometimes called hens and chicks.

This plant was prized throughout history, as the Romans and Greeks believed it to protect against thunderstorms. In the eighth century, Emperor Charlemagne decreed in his *Capitulare de Villis*—a governance guide for royal estates—that houseleeks be planted on every rooftop to ward off lightning strikes, fire, and evil.

Its scientific name means the "ever-living roof," derived from the Latin words *semper,* meaning "always;" *vivos,* meaning "to live;" and *tectum,* meaning "roof."

Some more of its many common names reflect this belief, such as *thunderplant* in English, and *Donnerbart,* meaning "Thor's beard" in German.

Houseleek may offer only mythical protection against elemental scorches, but its leaves contain juices that have actual anti-inflammatory properties and can be used to treat physical scorches on burned and swollen skin.

This shrubby plant is native to North America and commonly found across central and northern areas, growing in sunny, moist places. It changes appearance throughout the year, with oval green leaves and pale, frothy flowers in spring; followed by white, pea-size berries in the summer; and rust-colored leaves that are eventually shed in autumn. By winter, all that remains is a dazzling spray of solitary twigs, which turn a deep red, making them starkly vibrant against the frosty, pale landscape.

The *osier* part of its common name means "basket willow" or "wicker" in French, referencing its long branches, which are pliable and perfect for weaving beautiful containers and festive wreaths. They are best foraged in winter, when their burgundy color is at its brightest.

The *dogwood* part of its common name comes from the European variety *C. sanguinea*. Traditionally, British butchers used the hardened sticks to skewer meat for roasting. These were called *dags*, and the plant *dagwood,* which eventually became dogwood.

TURKEY TAIL
TRAMETES VERSICOLOR

This striking fungus can be found growing on fallen logs and tree stumps in forested areas across North America, Europe, and much of the Northern Hemisphere. It grows throughout the year but is most noticeable in winter when trees are bare and other plants die back. Each fungus grows in a thin, wavy rosette that spans 1 to 4 inches and often stacks in groups to create scaly, layered brackets.

These showy fans are striped on top in radiating tones of brown, beige, orange, and gray and have a velvety texture. The outer ring is often the palest, and its underside is also pale with very fine pores, not gills. It is this distinctive display that mimics the ostentatious plumage of a strutting turkey and lends this fungus its common name.

Quit ripping off my style!

The mushrooms can be collected and dried for floral arrangements, or added to terrariums and vivariums, while their tough, fibrous flesh can be pulped and used in papermaking.

MAIDENHAIR SPLEENWORT

ASPLENIUM TRICHOMANES

This common tufty fern grows all year long, nestled in the damp crevices of rocky habitats across temperate and subarctic areas around the world.

Evergreen fronds grow from a central rhizome on dark stems lined with small green leaflets. The whole plant grows in a spray, measuring 4 to 12 inches in diameter.

Its common name came about as a result of the doctrine of signatures, which was a concept adopted by early herbalists who selected plants to treat ailments based on the body parts the plants most resembled. For example, walnuts were believed to heal the brain, while mushrooms were a treatment for earache.

In summer, spleenwort leaves develop orange-brown spore pouches on their underside that resemble, you guessed it, a human spleen.

YELLOW BRAIN
TREMELLA MESENTERICA

Yellow brain is a peculiar fungus that grows all year long on fallen branches and tree stumps in the United Kingdom and temperate regions of the Americas, Asia, and Australia.

Yellow brain thrives in winter, when it appears on decaying surfaces. Its yellow-orange lobes grow in greasy, gelatinous folds, developing after a spell of rain and reaching up to an inch in diameter. The fungus will shrivel and shrink as it dries, becoming dark orange, papery, and hard, as it waits to be revived by subsequent rainfall.

This fungus does not feed directly on wood but instead lives parasitically, consuming crust fungi already present on rotting plants and detritus.

Hey, this branch is already taken!

It is also known as *witches' butter* because of its jellylike, translucent appearance.

Hocus-pocus breakfast time!

CHERRY LAUREL

PRUNUS LAUROCERASUS

Cherry laurel is an evergreen shrub native to southern Europe and Asia but widely naturalized in the United Kingdom. It has also naturalized in North America, where it is known as English laurel.

Cherry laurel grows along shady borders and woodland edges in dense bushes that reach 5 to 15 feet high. Its leaves are deep green and glossy with a fine-toothed edge, and their color persists all winter. In spring and summer cherry laurel blooms, producing erect stalks covered in creamy white flowers. By autumn, the pollinated flowers mature into dark burgundy berries, which are quickly snacked upon by birds.

Both the leaves and berries smell sweetly of almond when torn or crushed. But beware, this scent comes from the presence of highly toxic . . .

hydrogen cyanide!

Cherry laurel leaves are easily mistaken for culinary bay leaves, so don't accidentally add any to soups or stews . . . It could lead to an awkward end to your next dinner party.

Thank you for a lovely evening, Pam.

COMMON GORSE

ULEX EUROPAEUS

Common gorse is a hardy evergreen shrub, which is widespread in its native region of western Europe and an introduced species in the Americas, where it can be invasive. This plant grows on grasslands, heaths, and coastal areas in a spray of branches that reach 7 to 10 feet tall.

Common gorse is well armored with sharp, spiky leaves that cover its tangled stems, offering deep green color all year round. From winter onward, dense wands of sunshine-yellow, pealike flowers cover its branches, lighting up the dull landscape and emitting whiffs of coconut-like fragrance.

But don't sniff too eagerly, or your nose will pay!

OAKMOSS LICHEN

EVERNIA PRUNASTRI

This lichen can usually be found growing on oak trees, but it can also appear on other deciduous trees and conifers in woodlands and mountainous forests across the Northern Hemisphere. It grows all year round but is easiest to find in winter when much of the surrounding foliage has disappeared.

It grows in highly forked clusters, with thin, flat branches that clump together. As the common name suggests, this lichen is indeed mosslike in its appearance, with pale gray and sage-green coloration. It has a rough texture when dry but becomes rubbery and turns a darker olive green when wet.

Oakmoss has a long history of use in perfumery, where it provided the earthy, woody base for chypre-class fragrances. It has fallen out of favor in modern times, as oakmoss's aromatic essential oils can also cause skin irritation.

A purple dye can be made from this lichen by steeping it in ammonia to extract the bright pigment. It was also dried and powdered to scent Elizabethan wigs.

SHEPHERD'S PURSE

CAPSELLA BURSA-PASTORIS

This wild flowering weed can be found growing across the temperate Northern Hemisphere along roadsides and in lawns and pavement cracks. It grows in a low rosette of long, irregularly toothed leaves that persist all year. Shepherd's purse has tall, slender flowering stems that reach up to a foot high, producing clusters of tiny white flowers, which are quickly followed by distinctive, heart-shaped seedpods.

Do you accept . . . seeds?

These seedpods give shepherd's purse its common name, as they are said to look like the old coin pouches that were hung from belts in medieval times. Each pod is stuffed with tiny golden or copper-colored seeds that have a flattened oval shape. So these miniature purses even contain a stash of super-miniature coins.

The young leaves are edible and taste best when foraged early in winter, before the flowers start appearing. They can be eaten cooked or raw and have a mild peppery flavor.

In Asia, the plant is not considered a weed but is cultivated for food. In Chinese cuisine, it is called *jicai* and is added to stir-fries and wonton fillings. In Korea, it is known as *naengi*, and the whole young plant is blanched, nutty roots and all, to make a side dish or soup. In Japan, it is called *nazuna* and eaten in a rice dish during the January Festival of the Seven Herbs, which celebrates the valuable edible plants that grow in winter.

CHECKLIST

- ☐ Coltsfoot
- ☐ Daffodil
- ☐ Fuchsia-flowered gooseberry
- ☐ Alexanders
- ☐ Dutchman's-breeches
- ☐ Osoberry
- ☐ Common dandelion
- ☐ Wood sorrel
- ☐ Juniper haircap
- ☐ Black alder
- ☐ Agarita
- ☐ Wild primrose
- ☐ Dame's rocket
- ☐ Tulip tree
- ☐ Bloodroot
- ☐ Manroot
- ☐ Sweet violet
- ☐ Yellow fieldcap
- ☐ Lords-and-ladies
- ☐ Mountain laurel
- ☐ Common scurvy grass
- ☐ Ocotillo
- ☐ Bog myrtle
- ☐ Moschatel
- ☐ Stinking Benjamin
- ☐ Prairie smoke
- ☐ Thrift

SPRING

COLTSFOOT
TUSSILAGO FARFARA

Coltsfoot is a flowering plant, native to Europe and Asia, that grows on roadsides, riversides, wastelands, and disturbed soils. The plant can also be found across eastern and Atlantic coastal regions of North America, where it was introduced by settlers.

Bright-yellow coltsfoot flowers appear in spring, shooting up on scaly green stems with a reddish blush and felty hairs. They reach 3 to 12 inches tall and mature into fluffy white seed heads by the end of the season.

The common name "coltsfoot" refers to the horseshoe shape of its leaves.

Unusually, the leaves do not appear until after the flowers have bloomed, and as such, the plant is also known as:

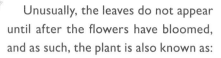

Son before the father

The *Tussilago* part of the plant's scientific name is derived from the Latin word *tussere*, meaning "to cough," as it was once an old European folk remedy for asthma and chest infections.

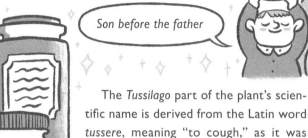

Coltsfoot is edible; both the flowers and leaves can be used to make a tea that has a licorice flavor, and the flowers can be used as an attractive garnish, tasting lightly of aniseed.

In Britain, the plant is still used to make an old-fashioned hard candy called:

Coltsfoot rock

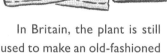

DAFFODIL
NARCISSUS

These iconic flowers are native to Europe but have naturalized in temperate regions around the world, including North America.

Daffodils are a sure sign of spring, when their bright green, strap-shaped leaves are among the first to emerge, breaking the surface of thawing soils. The plant grows on woodland and water edges, from an underground bulb with brown skin, which supports the hollow stem. Each stem bears a yellow, white, or occasionally orange flower, with six petals and a central cupped trumpet.

Hello there, handsome.

The *Narcissus* genus contains more than fifty flowering varieties and even more hybrids. This name comes from the way these flowers, which commonly grow near water, dip their heads and appear to gaze at their own reflection. This is reminiscent of Narcissus, from Greek mythology, who fell in love with his watery reflection.

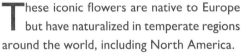

FUCHSIA-FLOWERED GOOSEBERRY

RIBES SPECIOSUM

This flowering shrub is native to California but cultivated in many regions as an ornamental. It grows up to 6 feet high in well-draining soils of chaparral thickets and shady canyon slopes, and blooms in early spring, when beautiful pendants of intensely red flowers dangle from its arching branches. The *speciosum* part of its classification means "showy" and "splendid," which it indeed is. But beware, as its glossy, lobed, and deeply green leaves look luscious but hide fiercely spiny thorns along its branches. These spines deter grazing and often snag animal hairs, which wild birds collect for building their nests.

The fruit matures in summer and is covered in bristles. It has a signature sour gooseberry taste. With the right amount of bravery—and gloves—the berries can be foraged and made into jams and syrups or added to pies and baked treats.

ALEXANDERS

SMYRNIUM OLUSATRUM

This wild flowering plant is native to the Mediterranean but grows abundantly across much of Europe, northern Africa, and western Asia. It can be found on coastal cliffs, roadsides, ancient ruins, and wastelands.

Alexanders are tall plants, reaching 5 to 6 feet high on reddish-green, stout stems that become ridged and hollow as they age. The flat, bright green leaves grow in threes at the end of succulent stalks that are wide and striped at their base. In spring, the plant produces small, greenish-yellow flowers on umbrellalike clusters. By autumn the globular green fruits mature and eventually ripen into grooved, black seedpods.

Alexanders were introduced outside their native region by the Greeks and Romans, who cultivated the plant as a food crop, as all parts are edible. It was known as:

The potherb of Alexandria

In spring, the tender stalks and stems taste like celery and can be eaten raw or added to soups and stews. The young leaves are similar to parsley and can be used as an herb or salad green. The budding flowers can be eaten like broccoli or pickled. In autumn, the peppery seeds can be dried and used as a spice. The roots can be roasted or boiled.

Alexanders are easily mistaken for similar species, particularly hemlock, which is extremely poisonous.

This plant's flowers have a pungent, musky aroma, like honey or myrrh. Its scientific name, *Smyrnium*, comes from the Greek word for "myrrh."

Horses love this plant and often graze on its tasty leaves. It is also known as horse parsley.

Snack time!

DUTCHMAN'S-BREECHES

DICENTRA CUCULLARIA

This unusual little plant grows across eastern and central North America, appearing in moist woodland areas, often near the base of a tree. The foliage emerges in early spring as a spray of finely fronded, feathery leaves that clump together, creating a small bush that can reach a foot or so in height. Delicate, pink-hued stalks arch up from the mass of foliage, bending slightly and bearing a dangling row of distinctive pendant flowers.

Uh, sorry . . . You caught me on laundry day.

These strange, pouchlike flowers are white, or occasionally pink, with creamy yellow lower lobes. Their shape is said to look like pairs of upturned, pillowy trousers, lending the wildflower its common name. This arrangement looks like a miniature washing line, hung with a woodland resident's petite laundry.

By the end of spring, the pollinated flowers develop into rice-shaped fruits full of tiny, kidney-shaped seeds, and the rest of the plant dies back to its bulbous, pink tubers.

OSOBERRY

OEMLERIA CERASIFORMIS

This tall, fruiting shrub is native to North America and usually grows 10 to 15 feet high along roadsides, stream banks, and forest edges throughout the Pacific coastal region. It is among the first plants to leaf and blossom in spring, marking the start of the season.

Red-tinged buds appear on the reddish-brown branches, revealing bunches of lush, green, narrow leaves that point upward when young and smell like cucumber when crushed. These are accompanied by pendants of white flowers, which dangle below the leaves like showy candelabras.

By the end of spring the leaves are fully grown, spreading out on arching branches. The pollinated flowers on female trees produce hanging fruits that grow on pink stems—at first small and green, then turning orange and finally blue-black when ripe. The olive-size, plum-shaped berries are dined on by birds, squirrels, foxes, coyotes, deer, and raccoons, but it is the hungry bears that lend it their name, as *oso* means "bear" in Spanish.

COMMON DANDELION

TARAXACUM OFFICINALE

These iconic wildflowers appear in spring and are ubiquitous across much of the world, particularly North America and Europe. They are opportunists, growing almost anywhere their seeds settle, from urban pavement cracks and empty lots to rural pastures and nature trails. As such, dandelions often appear where they're not wanted and can be regarded as a weed.

The foliage appears first, forming a rounded spray of leaves approximately 8 to 20 inches in diameter. Each leaf is long and hairless, with a thick central midvein. The leaves' edges are deeply lobed, a shape well described by the plant's common name, which derives from the French *dent-de-lion*, meaning "lion's tooth."

Each flower grows singly on a smooth and hollow round stem that rises 4 to 12 inches above the leafy base. The flower is first clasped in thin green bracts, which create a tight, cylindrical bud that eventually opens to reveal a multitude of tiny florets inside. The many florets collectively appear as a golden-yellow pom-pom, which opens in the day and closes at night.

The flowers mature into a spherical puffball of fluffy, silvery seeds that disperse on the wind like tiny parachutes. In Britain, this seed head is called a dandelion clock, because of a folk tradition where you blow away the seeds to supposedly reveal the time of day. Depending on the region, this was determined either by how many puffs of breath it took to completely remove the seeds, or by the number of seeds remaining after one big breath.

Dandelions can be admired or reviled, but either way they're a fascinating plant. The whole plant is edible in small amounts: the leaves can be used as a spring green, eaten raw or sautéed. The buds can be preserved in brine and enjoyed like capers. The flowers can be used to flavor wines, teas, and cordials. Even the fleshy taproot can be cooked like a root vegetable or dried, roasted, and brewed like coffee.

The hollow stem releases a milky, white sap when broken, which contains latex and can be cultivated to produce natural rubber. Because of this, dandelions are known as *mælkebøtte* in Danish, meaning "milk bin," and in Lithuanian they are *pienė*, meaning "milky."

Dandelions also have a long history of medicinal and herbal use. Most notably, the leaves and roots were dried and taken as a diuretic, which inspired the exceptionally descriptive old English folk name of:

Pissabed

Mmm, delicious. What tea is this again?

Many similar subspecies of dandelion exist and can be difficult to distinguish. These are often classified under the general banner of *T. officinale*.

WOOD SORREL
OXALIS ACETOSELLA

These iconic flowers are native to Europe but have naturalized in temperate regions around the world, including North America.

In spring, a creeping mat of trefoil, cloverlike leaves appear on tangled stalks that form clumps. The flowers follow, with five white petals, veined with pale pink or purple stripes.

Both the leaves and flowers of wood sorrel fold up like fans at night.

The scientific name, *Oxalis acetosella*, is derived from Greek words meaning "sour," "sharp," and "acidic." As these words suggest, the leaves have a bright, lemony flavor when eaten. Edible in small amounts, the leaves can be used raw to make refreshing iced tea and mock lemonade, or dried and used as a curdling agent in cheese making.

O. acetosella is widespread in Europe and Asia but rarer in North America. The closely related and visually similar *O. montana* is the prevalent North American species, which is also known as wood sorrel.

Other North American species are yellow wood sorrel (*O. stricta*) and violet wood sorrel (*O. violacea*), which share characteristics with other *Oxalis* species, though their flowers are yellow and lavender, respectively.

JUNIPER HAIRCAP
POLYTRICHUM JUNIPERINUM

This striking evergreen moss can be found growing on every continent, but particularly in the Northern Hemisphere, where it favors mineral-rich soils and dry, rocky places in cool forests, dunes, and grasslands. It commonly appears on previously burned areas as a pioneer plant alongside fireweed (page 98).

Juniper haircap grows in dense, ground-covering mats comprised of spiked upright fronds, which are bright green with reddish-brown bases. In spring, it is easy to spot because of the reddish-orange, starry rosettes that appear at the tips of each frond. These aren't flowers but the male reproductive part of the moss. The female parts grow on separate plants, on thin, red stalks that stretch above their base like ethereal tendrils. Each stalk is tipped with a small, beaked spore sac that becomes hairy and hooded as it matures, hence the "haircap" name.

As this moss is evergreen, insects and beetles use it as a valuable year-round food source. Songbirds use the wiry red stems in the construction of their nests, and perhaps make a snack of the insects within, too. A one-stop shop for songbirds.

BLACK ALDER

ALNUS GLUTINOSA

Black alder is a deciduous tree native to Europe, northern Africa, and temperate Asia. It is also widespread in North America, where it was introduced by settlers. The tree grows in moist soils, mixed woodlands, or near water, reaching 30 to 90 feet high.

Black alder trees have straight trunks with dark, fissured bark, speckled gray branches, and loosely conical crowns. In winter the branches bear showy, red-purple buds that develop into beautiful flowers and catkins by spring, accompanied by broadly oval leaves.

Male catkins begin as thin, green tubes that sprout upward before flowering and dangling off like little yellow tails. Female catkins are green and oval, maturing over summer before hardening into woody cones that release tiny, winged seeds in autumn.

When cut, black alder wood turns from pale to orange or red, giving the impression of a bloody wound. As such, in British folklore, the tree was associated with bad luck.

Natural pigments can be extracted from the catkins and sap, yielding a green dye used by sneaky outlaws and witches to make camouflaged garments.

Black alder timber is soft when first cut but becomes very durable when wet. The timber is also resistant to underwater rot. Much of Venice is built upon stilts of black alder.

AGARITA
BERBERIS TRIFOLIOLATA

This evergreen shrub can be found in southwestern North America and northern Mexico, where it grows in sprawling thickets on rocky slopes and cliffs. Its tangled stems are covered in grayish-green, widely spiked leaves that grow in groups of three—a foliage as dangerous as it looks, stiffly sharp and tipped with spines.

You snooze, you lose.

In early spring it buds and blooms with fragrant yellow flowers, which ripen into dazzling red berries. If you're intrepid enough to brave the dangerous, leafy armor, you will be rewarded with edible fruits that have a tart, slightly sweet taste. They can be crushed or boiled to extract their juices for making jellies and wines, or added whole to chutneys and pies. But don't leave it too late—these tasty berries also attract hungry birds, whom you'll be competing with.

Agarita branches and roots can be harvested to make a natural yellow dye. When chopped and steeped in water, they release a bright, sunny pigment, used by some Indigenous nations to add color to basketry, weavings, and hides.

AGARITA

WILD PRIMROSE

PRIMULA VULGARIS

This pretty spring wildflower appears in damp, sheltered habitats such as forest clearings and waysides. It is native to Europe but has been introduced in North America as an ornamental addition to woodlands and cottage gardens.

Wild primrose produces creamy yellow flowers on short stems, which nestle in a rosette of fat, wrinkled green leaves. Its name comes from the Latin phrase *prima rosa*, meaning "first rose," and although it isn't a rose, it is one of the first flowers to appear in spring.

In European folklore wild primroses are synonymous with fairies. It was said that if you hung the flowers above your door, fairies would bless your house. Eating them meant you might even see one!

DAME'S ROCKET

HESPERIS MATRONALIS

This herbaceous plant is native to Eurasia but can be found across most of the world, including North America, where it has been cultivated for its pretty, scented flowers. It is undemanding and hardy, growing in prairies, woodlands, hedgerows, waste grounds, and roadsides, with pointed, toothed leaves that are covered in fine hairs. Dame's rocket first appears as a leafy rosette, then flowers in its second year.

First-year basal rosette

In late spring, tall stems rise from the base, producing clusters of four-petalled purple and white flowers. These have a sweet, violet-like scent, which is strongest in the evening.

The *Hesperis* part of its official classification means "of the evening." *Matronalis* refers to the Roman festival Matronalia, which was dedicated to Juno, the goddess of motherhood, and celebrated married women, mature matrons, and dames. It took place on March 1, when these flowers begin to bloom.

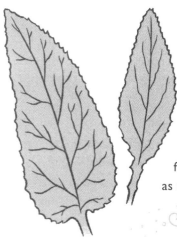

Dame's rocket is from the same family as broccoli, mustard, and arugula and, like its plant siblings, is edible. The young, vitamin-rich leaves have a peppery, spicy flavor similar to arugula, which is also known as rocket in Britain.

Older leaves and unopened buds can be harvested and cooked like spring greens. The flowering stems are great for cutting and bringing indoors, where they will fill a room with their fragrance. If this plant is invasive in your area, foraging and cutting before it goes to seed will also stop it spreading—it's a win-win!

TULIP TREE
LIRIODENDRON TULIPIFERA

This beautiful tree grows in eastern parts of North America. It can reach up to 100 feet high, growing on a straight trunk with a wide, covering canopy of distinctive bright green, four-pointed starry leaves. Some say the leaves look like the body of a violin, which lends it another common name, fiddle tree. These leaves first appear as red buds in spring and grow to 6 inches or more across before turning shades of gold in autumn and then shedding.

The tulip tree produces striking cup-shaped flowers, which appear from mid to late spring, depending on the region, and bloom into summer. The flowers have six pale greenish-yellow petals with flashes of orange at their base. They resemble tulips, magnolias, or lilies, and this likeness is reflected not only in the tulip tree's common name but also its official classification: *Liriodendron* is Greek for "lily tree," and *tulipifera* means "tulip bearing."

The flowers tend to bloom on higher branches, so you may need to admire them from afar. They are full of nectar and loved by hummingbirds and honeybees. At their peak, the flowers are so full of sugary liquid that on breezy days they can overflow and drip onto unsuspecting picnickers below.

BLOODROOT
SANGUINARIA CANADENSIS

This wildflower can be found in woodland thickets, floodplains, and rivers' edges across central and eastern North America. Each flower grows from a lone stalk, wrapped with a single leaf that gently cups an emerging bud prior to opening. After the flower has bloomed, the leaf unfurls into a large green fan with deeply scalloped edges, a wrinkly surface, and a grayish underside.

Bloodroot stalks reach 6 to 10 inches high and are tipped with flowers that have eight to twelve white petals and yellow centers full of stamens. The flowers open to greet the sunshine and close as daylight wanes.

The grisly common name is reflected in its genus name, *Sanguinaria*, which means "blood" or "bleeding." This originates from the plant's subterranean rhizome, which is fleshy, juicy, and red when cut.

The bright liquid from the rhizomes can be extracted and used to dye textiles, leather, and woven crafts a vibrant orange. But beware: its intimidating name is warranted, as the plant is toxic—so make sure to wear protective equipment if you decide to interact with it.

MANROOT

MARAH FABACEA

This flowering vine is native to the West Coast of North America and northern Mexico, where it grows by streams and on embankments. In early spring, hairy stems appear from tuberous, subterranean roots and sprawl across the ground, finding other plants and structures to climb. Large, lobed leaves grow from the reaching stems, accompanied in late spring by a stalk of small, white, star-shaped flowers. These mature into green, golf ball–size fruits covered in spikes.

Manroot's common name comes from the lumpy, tan-colored roots that rupture the surface of the soil. These huge roots can reach several feet long, with extending limbs that can at first appear to be those of buried remains.

Although there are a number of regional manroot species with similar properties and appearances, this variety is the most common. Another name for the plant is wild cucumber, the reason for which is more evident in these other varieties such as *M. oreganus*, which has a cucumberlike striped green fruit with fewer spines.

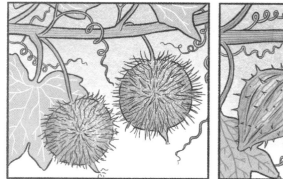

M. fabacea

M. oreganus

Contrary to the edible-sounding name, all parts of this plant can be toxic to humans. *Marah fabacea* is particularly interesting because its toxicity was sometimes used by hunters from Indigenous nations, who crushed the roots and tossed them into fishing pools. This released toxic saponins into the water, which caused nearby fish to become stunned and float to the surface, making for an easy mealtime.

So cucumbers might be off the menu, but the fish is a specialty.

Sweet violets bloom in spring at the edges of forests and meadows or nestled under shady hedgerows. They are originally native to Europe but are also found in North America, Asia, and Australia.

The low-growing plant produces small, delicate flowers that are usually deep purple but can occasionally be blue or white. The blooms are highly fragrant, with a distinctive softly floral, powdery aroma. They are often picked and given as love tokens. The heart-shaped leaves bring some additional romance.

Sweet violets have many historic and contemporary uses; their characteristic scent has been used to make perfumes and soaps, while the edible flowers can be added to liqueurs, candies, and cakes.

YELLOW FIELDCAP

BOLBITIUS TITUBANS

This small, fragile mushroom is widespread across Europe and North America, where it grows in highly fertilized soils. It appears in spring, often in fields populated by cows or scattered with cut hay, and thrives on the rich dung and decaying straw.

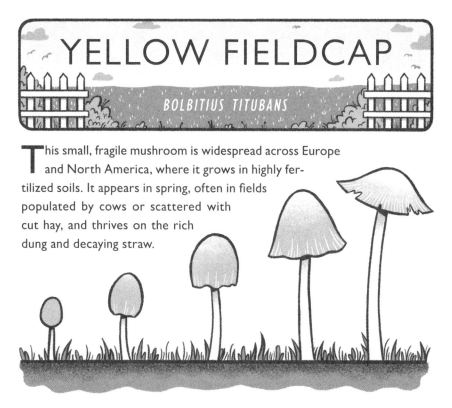

Yellow fieldcaps have a very short life cycle. They begin as bright yellow, slimy bulbs held atop short stems, and eventually become taller white umbrellas with vertical striation and exposed brown gills on their underside. This growth can happen over the course of a single day, with mature mushrooms reaching 1 to 4 inches high.

Because the young cap presents as a shiny yellow oval, this mushroom is also known as:

Egg yolk fungus

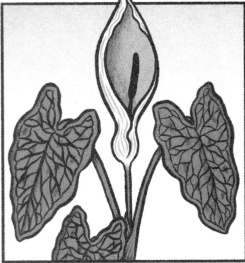

This unusual woodland plant is native to Europe but also found in North America, where it was introduced as an ornamental and subsequently spread into the wild.

In spring, the green waxy leaves of lords-and-ladies appear in low-growing bunches in moist, shady areas. The arrow-shaped leaves unfurl, reaching 8 to 10 inches in length, and are sometimes spotted with dark purple blotches.

The flowers follow the leaves and are held above the foliage on fleshy stems. They have a large, tear-shaped, pale green sheath, which is sometimes blushed with burgundy. This lily-like hood protects the flowering parts and contains a purple-black, wand-shaped spadix.

This flowering structure is an elaborate flytrap. It generates a pungent smell and emits heat to attract midges and flies, which aid pollination.

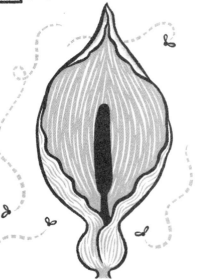

This plant has a lot of alternative and saucy common names:

Say what?

Adam & Eve, priest's pintle, naked girls, and willy lily

Almost all are cheeky innuendos based on its resemblance to genitalia. This is a stark contrast to the pious nuns in fifteenth-century English abbeys, who harvested the root to starch their altar cloths and communion linens.

It's likely that you will find this plant in poison gardens, as all parts contain irritants and toxins.

In autumn, the fertilized flower develops into a scepter of bright red berries that cause serious irritation and inflammation of the mouth and throat if eaten. There is no known antidote to *A. maculatum* poisoning.

MOUNTAIN LAUREL

KALMIA LATIFOLIA

Mountain laurel is a common sight on rocky slopes and forested areas of eastern North America. This shrub grows in bushy thickets with many branched stems and reaches 6 to 10 feet high, sometimes taller if isolated. The glossy, deep green leaves are present all year round.

In late spring, flat clusters of crinkled pink buds appear, resembling dots of piped cake frosting. These open to reveal bowl-shaped flowers that range from white and pastel pink to magenta and burgundy. The flower shape is geometric and looks distinctively like an upturned umbrella.

Hey, quit it!

Mountain laurel has unusual kinetic anthers, which are dark tipped and held under tension against the petals. When a bee visits these flowers, the anthers are disturbed and triggered, springing forward like a mousetrap, dusting the bee's back with pollen and aiding fertilization.

Mountain laurel is toxic to humans and animals, but the timber can be used for crafting and carving, particularly for making utensils—hence its occasional nickname, spoonwood.

COMMON SCURVY GRASS

COCHLEARIA OFFICINALIS

This flowering herb can be found in rocky, salty soils of coastal regions and marshes across northern and western Europe, where it grows in small, messy clumps ranging from 3 inches to a foot high. The succulent, heart-shaped green leaves grow on hairless stems connected at a central base. In late spring, brilliant white or mauve flowers appear, clustered at the ends of rising stalks.

Stocking up on the good stuff!

The plant gets its common name because sailors would forage and eat it to prevent scurvy—its natural coastal habitat making it conveniently placed for departing mariners. The leaves have a bitter, sharp taste that is a result of their high vitamin C content.

In the nineteenth century, until the discovery of lemons and citrus fruits supplanted it, common scurvy grass was a popular plant, recommended by herbalists and loved by seafarers. It was eaten raw in sandwiches or dried and brewed into a tonic or ale. For a short while in history, it had a free ticket to travel the world and was thus distributed and naturalized in many temperate coastal regions, including North America.

Common Scurvy Grass

SCURVY TONIC

OCOTILLO
FOUQUIERIA SPLENDENS

This spindly, desert plant thrives in dry, rocky regions of the southwestern United States and northern Mexico, where it can grow up to 20 feet tall. It is well adapted to drought and spends much of the year looking like an abandoned arrangement of gray, dead, prickly twigs.

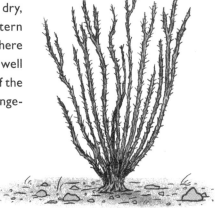

But after rainfall, the plant awakens, sprouting lots of small, fleshy-green leaves along its stems. In spring it blooms a spire of bright red, tubular flowers, which cluster at the tip of each stem, and it may flower again in summer, depending on additional rainfall.

The common name comes from the Nahuatl word *ocotl*, meaning "torch made of pine," referencing its flame-like inflorescence. Other common names include:

Desert coral and candlewood

Ocotillo has a multitude of uses. The long stems are hardy and can be trimmed to make beautiful walking canes, or pruned and used as fencing poles, which often take root after cutting to create a living, thorny border that keeps out intruders. The flowers are edible and can be enjoyed as a tangy snack or colorful garnish, or dried and steeped in hot water to make a delicious tisane. The bark and roots have many folk medicinal uses across different cultures, from a poultice to stop bleeding to a dried infusion said to relieve fatigue.

BOG MYRTLE

MYRICA GALE

This short, bushy plant grows, as its name suggests, in boggy areas such as marshes and wetlands across northern Europe and eastern parts of North America. It can grow 2 to 5 feet tall but often stays small, as grazing animals eat the fragrant leaves, stunting its growth.

In spring, the bare, reddish-brown branches bud with leaves and colorful catkins, which are either male or female. Male plants produce yellow cones with red scales that open to expose delicate stamens. Female plants produce smaller catkins that start as golden or rust-colored buds and open into a spray of red stigmas.

Male catkins

Female catkins

The deep-green foliage matures into narrow, oval leaves that have a slightly pointed tip. These give off a pleasantly herbal, resinous aroma when crushed and are a natural insect repellent, valued in the Highlands of Scotland to ward off hungry midges.

The aromatic leaves are also used to flavor teas, gins, beers, and liqueurs, while the catkins can be boiled to release a waxy coating used to make candles, balms, and cosmetics.

66

MOSCHATEL

ADOXA MOSCHATELLINA

This wildflower can be found throughout much of the Northern Hemisphere and is especially common in the United Kingdom and northern regions of North America. It grows in colonies of multiple plants, which reach 6 to 8 inches tall in shady and moist woodland habitats.

In spring, erect stems topped with unusual cube-shaped flowers reach above the lower herbaceous leaves. These boxy blooms measure $\frac{1}{4}$ to $\frac{1}{2}$ inch across and are comprised of four pale green flowers facing outward at right angles to each other and a fifth on top, looking skyward.

This tall, structural floral arrangement is the origin of its British common name, town hall clock.

Another name is:

Five-faced bishop

STINKING BENJAMIN
❧ *TRILLIUM ERECTUM* ❧

Many varieties of *Trillium* are found across North America, from the large, white *T. grandiflorum* in eastern areas to the drooping *T. cernuum* found in the north to the tiny *T. nivale* in the Midwest. They all have similar leaf and flower characteristics, but the wild *T. erectum* is especially fascinating. It grows in the moist, rich soils of forest floors in eastern areas from early spring, where it takes advantage of the sparse canopy that gives it extra sunlight before any taller neighbors wake up.

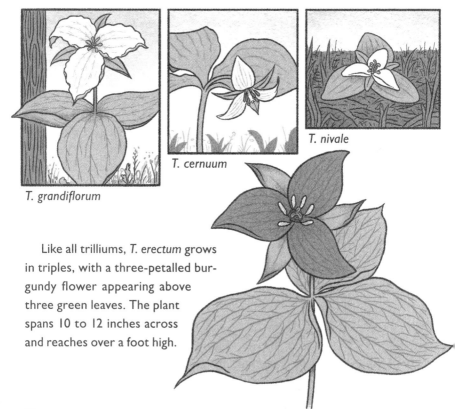

T. nivale

T. cernuum

T. grandiflorum

Like all trilliums, *T. erectum* grows in triples, with a three-petalled burgundy flower appearing above three green leaves. The plant spans 10 to 12 inches across and reaches over a foot high.

Stinking Benjamin's off-putting common name comes from the flower's scent, which unpleasantly mimics the stench of rotting meat. The flower's pungent aroma, combined with its blood red color, attracts carrion flies, which visit the flower, brush against the white stamens, and pollinate the plant.

And this is going to help, right?

Surely! It stinks as much as you, Benjamin.

The visceral connections don't stop there, as the crimson petals were utilized by medieval folk herbalists who followed the doctrine of signatures, "treating like with like," so poultices of this smelly plant would be applied to equally gory and reeking wounds, ulcers, and gangrene.

The root of this plant was used by some Indigenous nations to induce childbirth and aid labor, so it became known as birth root, which over time also became bethroot.

PRAIRIE SMOKE
GEUM TRIFLORUM

This distinctive North American wild-flower can be found in western and northern regions of the United States and much of Canada, where it grows in sandy prairies and on gravelly mountain foothills.

In early spring, toothy, fern-like leaves appear, growing in a low rosette. Then, in late spring, hairy, reddish stalks rise up to a foot tall, each producing a pretty trio of nodding, pink flowers.

After pollination in summer, the flowers turn upward and erupt into plumes of feathery seed heads, ready to disperse on the wind. The fluffy torches are a silvery mauve, fading to white or gold in autumn, and earn the plant its common name, as they cover the landscape with a hazy cloud of softness.

THRIFT
ARMERIA MARITIMA

This pretty coastal wildflower can be spotted blooming from spring onward throughout the Northern Hemisphere. It grows where few other plants survive: dry, sandy habitats and salt marshes near the coast.

Thrift has a tufted, grassy base of simple green leaves, from which long flowering stems emerge, tipped with pink pom-pom blooms.

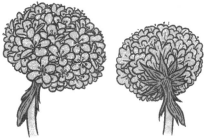

Its species name, *maritima*, and alternate common name, sea pink, are each descriptive of its habitat and appearance.

Thrift was featured on the design of a British threepenny coin in use from 1937 to 1952. A pocket reminder to spend money wisely.

Keep it thrifty!

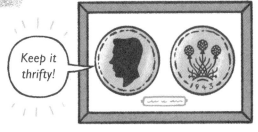

☀ CHECKLIST ☀

- ☐ Wild bee balm
- ☐ Honey locust
- ☐ Arrowhead
- ☐ Foxglove
- ☐ Elder
- ☐ Greater burdock
- ☐ Hooded ladies' tresses
- ☐ Gold of pleasure
- ☐ Common puffball
- ☐ Grass-of-parnassus
- ☐ Teasel
- ☐ Yarrow
- ☐ Pipe vine
- ☐ Bird's-foot trefoil
- ☐ Pearly everlasting
- ☐ Bracken
- ☐ Fireweed
- ☐ Wild marjoram
- ☐ Great yellow pond lily
- ☐ Viper's bugloss
- ☐ Blanketflower
- ☐ Soapwort
- ☐ Yellow rattle
- ☐ Common cattail
- ☐ Devil's-fig

SUMMER

WILD BEE BALM

MONARDA FISTULOSA

Wild bee balm is a showy wildflower native to North America, where it covers almost the whole continent. It grows in versatile conditions but generally favors well-draining soils in rocky woodlands, prairies, borders, and roadsides.

It appears in spring, growing in bushy clumps with toothy, pointed leaves. The foliage is green but sometimes blushed with pink and is arranged on erect stems. In summer, the branches can reach 3 to 4 feet tall and are topped with striking purple or lilac blooms—a shaggy arrangement of tubular petals clustered above a green bract. Its common name reflects these nectar-rich flowers, which attract a lot of bees.

The aromatic leaves can be foraged and used as an herb, in salsas, salads, and pestos. When crushed, they also release fragrant oils that are a natural mosquito repellent—though they can cause skin irritation, so handle cautiously if you have sensitive skin.

It brings the bees but kicks out the mosquitos—what a star!

Great tea, just not THAT tea!

Owing to its similar aroma, wild bee balm is sometimes called wild bergamot, but it is not the same as the bergamot citrus used in Earl Grey tea. However, the fresh and dried flowers and leaves can be added to teas, tinctures, and cocktails to give them a fragrant, herby twist.

Wild bee balm has a history of use in folk medicine, most notably as a treatment for toothache and gingivitis. Interestingly, the plant does contain the chemical thymol, an active ingredient used in modern mouthwashes.

Other varieties of bee balm have red, pink, or white flowers and produce a range of aromas, from herbal to citrus, but *M. fistulosa* is the most widespread wild variety.

HONEY LOCUST
GLEDITSIA TRIACANTHOS

This tree grows in central and southern areas of North America in the moist soil of woodland edges and river valleys. It can grow over 60 feet high, with a thorny bark and arching branches covered in delicate rows of yellow-green leaves.

Honey locust trees blossom in late spring with small yellow-white flowers. By summer these develop into large seedpods that curve and twist, hanging in loose spirals. As they mature, the green seedpods turn golden yellow and brown and range from 6 to 12 inches long. Encased in the pods are seeds surrounded by an oozing, sugary pulp that lends this tree its delicious name.

The tender, young pods are edible and can be cooked as a legume. The mature seeds can also be roasted and then steeped to make a tasty beverage, or dried and ground to make a sweet flour.

This tree is covered in exceptionally large thorns, which are initially red and then turn black and viciously sharp when mature. They're so tough that they have been used as natural tailoring pins and nails. *Triacanthos* means "three thorns" in Greek.

ARROWHEAD

SAGITTARIA SAGITTIFOLIA

Arrowhead is an aquatic plant with a native range across Europe, Siberia, and China. In spring the arrow-shaped, glossy green foliage appears above the surface of shallow ponds and wetlands. Each leaf is 2 to 3 inches long, supported on flat stalks that reach 1 to 2 feet high.

In summer, flowering stems reach upward, bearing round, reddish buds that reveal small, white blooms with a purple center.

After flowering, the whole plant dies back and leaves a submerged, cherry bomb–shaped bulb that waits patiently for spring. These bulbs are starchy and edible, lending the plant another common name:

Swamp potato

In North America, *S. sagittifolia* can be found in eastern wetlands but is regarded as invasive. Broadleaf arrowhead (*S. latifolia*) is a North American native species, which has very similar characteristics to its Eurasian sibling, including the charming and equally starchy alternative name:

Duck potato

77

FOXGLOVE
DIGITALIS PURPUREA

This iconic wildflower can be found growing on roadside verges and woodland edges throughout summer. It is native to Europe but has been introduced in many temperate regions around the world, including in North America, where it has naturalized.

Foxgloves grow from a base of oval leaves that spiral around the stem. The lower leaves are wrinkly and covered in soft, downy hairs. Upper leaves are smaller and simpler. The flowering stem can reach 3 to 6 feet high and supports rows of trumpet-shaped, pendant blooms at its apex. The hollow flowers can reach 2 inches long; are pink, purple, or white in color; and are often speckled inside with burgundy spots.

The *Digitalis* part of this plant's scientific name refers to human digits, which the thimble-shaped flowers fit so perfectly.

Sweet mitts!

The common name comes from an old medieval belief that "fairy folk" would use the flowers as mittens, so they were called "folk's gloves," which became foxglove.

As pretty and quaint as this wildflower appears, all parts of the plant are poisonous. Despite its toxicity, *Digitalis* has a long history of medicinal use by herbalists, who used it to treat heart conditions. However, if the dose was not carefully monitored, ingestion could prove fatal. This danger is reflected in another common name:

Dead man's bells

This shrubby tree is native to Eurasia and North Africa, commonly found in sunny hedgerows and woodland edges, or along roadsides and waste places. It is also common in North America, where it is known as black elder.

Elder grows from a multistemmed trunk, in bushy sprays that reach 10 to 25 feet tall. In spring, scaly buds appear on the greenish branches and mature into pointed leaves with serrated edges.

In summer, elder is glorious in bloom, covered in frothy umbrellas of creamy white flowers that measure 2 to 5 inches across.

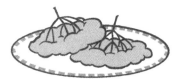

Elderflowers have a musky fragrance and are edible. They can be foraged to flavor syrups, wines, and teas. The whole flower head can be battered and fried to make fritters, which are a common addition to Scandinavian Midsummer feasts.

By the end of summer, the pale floral umbrellas ripen into pink-stemmed sprays of purple-black shiny berries. The berries are toxic if eaten raw but are safe to eat when cooked and sweetened, becoming earthy, spiced, and fruity in flavor. They make fantastic cordials, jams, and pies.

In ancient Europe, the elder tree was embedded in folklore, long regarded as sacred and magical. Druids believed the Elder Mother deity lived within its heartwood and that she would haunt anyone taking a branch without permission. As such, furniture made from elder was said to be unlucky and cursed.

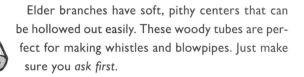

Elder branches have soft, pithy centers that can be hollowed out easily. These woody tubes are perfect for making whistles and blowpipes. Just make sure you *ask first*.

GREATER BURDOCK

ARCTIUM LAPPA

This large-leafed plant is native to Eurasia but has naturalized across northern parts of North America and can be found growing along roadsides, woodland edges, and waste grounds. It is biennial, appearing first as a wide rosette of wrinkly leaves with wavy edges and red-tinted stems. It then flowers in the summer of its second year, with tall, branching stems topped with thistlelike globes and purple petals that reach over 6 feet tall.

This spiky flower acts like the burrs of its common name, attaching readily to the fur and clothing of annoyed passersby. In fact, the unique shape of these sticky spikes directly inspired the invention of Velcro.

Greater burdock grows from a long taproot that is best harvested before the plant flowers. It is used in the cuisines of many cultures. In Japan, this root is finely sliced and sautéed with carrot to make a savory dish called *kinpira gobo*. In Britain, it is used as a flavoring in the herbal soda Dandelion & Burdock.

HOODED LADIES' TRESSES

SPIRANTHES ROMANZOFFIANA

This wild orchid is native to North America, Ireland, and the United Kingdom, where it appears along rivers, marshes, and wet meadows. It grows from a base of long, narrow leaves that point upward on an erect stem, and in summer, it produces a flowering stalk, 4 to 12 inches tall. The creamy white flowers are held on a green spike, densely arranged in vertical rows, which twist in a geometric display.

It is from this spiraling bloom that the plant derives its scientific name *Spiranthes*, from the Greek words *speira*, meaning "coil," and *anthos*, meaning "flower."

The individual flowers resemble tiny hooded bonnets, worn by women at the time of the plant's discovery and naming. The *tresses* part of its common name refers to the budding, flowering spike, which resembles a braided tress of hair.

GOLD OF PLEASURE

CAMELINA SATIVA

This flowering plant can be found growing, either wild or cultivated, across Europe, Asia, and North America and into the Southern Hemisphere. Its flourishing success is due to a high tolerance of drought, frost, and poor soil conditions.

It grows 1 to 3 feet high, on slightly hairy, branching stems with alternate, lance-shaped leaves that are stalkless. In summer, the upper stems are covered in small, pale yellow flowers on individual stalks, which cluster together in a rounded crown.

As summer wanes, each pollinated flower matures into a small fruit capsule. Inside each of these are the orange-brown seeds for which gold of pleasure is prized and cultivated, as they are edible and rich in vitamins and omega-3 fatty acids.

Archaeological evidence from European dig sites can date the plant's use as an agricultural crop as far back as the Bronze Age.

I've got a great breakfast recipe you're gonna love.

Gold of pleasure seeds were found inside the stomach of the mummified Tollund Man, an Iron Age Scandinavian who lived during fourth century BC. Researchers also found barley and flax, suggesting his last meal was some kind of nutritious, seedy porridge.

This ancient seed is now seeing a resurgence in popularity as a superfood grain, cooking oil, and renewable biofuel.

COMMON PUFFBALL
LYCOPERDON PERLATUM

Common puffball is a mushroom that grows around the world in fields and woodland clearings.

In summer the young fungus appears, white and bulblike, studded with tiny conical spines. As the mushroom matures, it grows taller, from 1 to 3 inches high, becoming an inverted pear shape.

Older mushrooms turn a dull brown and shed some of their spines, leaving shallow pockmarks. Inside the maturing head, spores ripen and pressurize until a drop of rain or falling twig ruptures the surface. This kinetic action releases a plume of spore gas into the air.

Common puffballs are edible, but only when they are young and if the flesh inside is completely white. As the mushroom ages and darkens, it becomes poisonous.

Hey buddy, want a bump? Heh heh.

The spores of this mushroom can be damaging if inhaled, sometimes even fatal. This has lent the common puffball an evil alternate name:

The devil's-snuffbox

I'm so very sorry.

The scientific name of this mushroom is a delight. In Greek, *lyco* means "wolf," and *perdon* means "to break wind." When you put those beauties together, you get some bona fide . . .

wolf farts

GRASS-OF-PARNASSUS

PARNASSIA

This distinctive wildflower can be found in wet meadows, marshes, and mountains across temperate regions of the Northern Hemisphere.

It grows from a base of heart-shaped green leaves that support long stems of up to a foot that bear buds in summer. The white flowers are saucer shaped, with five petals distinctively striped with translucent veins, cupped around yellow, green, or pinkish centers.

The plant is named after Mount Parnassus in Greece, the ancient home of the mythological Muses. There are two stories as to the origin of this name. Some say the plant was loved by the cattle that grazed on the mountainside and thus became an honorary grass. Others suggest Carl Linnaeus, an eighteenth-century taxonomist, loved the flower so much that he named it after the majestic mountain.

The plant has another common name, which is considerably less romantic but no less spectacular:

Bog star

TEASEL
DIPSACUS FULLONUM

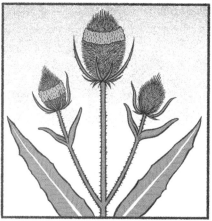

This tall, barbed plant is native to Eurasia and North Africa but also common in North America and Australasia, where it was introduced by settlers. It can be found along roads and waterways, or in pastures and abandoned lots.

Teasel grows from a rosette of puckered and spiked leaves at its base, supporting a robust and upright flowering stem that reaches 4 to 8 feet high. In summer thistlelike spiny eggs appear atop the branching stalks, covered in tiny, densely packed purple blooms. The whole plant is covered with prickles, from stem and leaf to stalk and flower head. In autumn the plant dries out, leaving a brown, woody skeleton that often remains standing throughout winter.

The *Dipsacus* part of its scientific name comes from *dipsa*, the Greek word for "thirst." This is because the upper leaves of teasel, which are arranged in pairs, fuse together around the stem to create an enclosed cup that collects rainwater.

Textile makers use dried teasel flower heads as natural combs to improve the durability and texture of woven fabrics and woolen fibers.

Yarrow is a common wild-flower that can be found growing in grasslands, verges, and meadows across the Northern Hemisphere. It grows in an upright fashion, with a central stem, bearing alternately arranged and delicately fronded leaves that are easy to identify.

In some Spanish-speaking regions the plant is called *plumajillo*, which means "little feather," or *milenrama*, meaning "many branches." This naming convention is continued in its scientific name, *millefolium*, meaning "thousand leaves."

It flowers from June to September, with flat-topped clusters of creamy white or sometimes pink flowers.

Yarrow has many historic medicinal uses, which account for its wide distribution. In particular, it was used to treat wounds and staunch bleeding, leading to its other common names:

Herba militaris, staunchweed, and knight's milfoil

The *Achillea* part of its classification comes from Greek legends of the Trojan War, where it is said that Achilles took the plant with him into battle to aid fallen soldiers.

In the Middle Ages, yarrow was used by brewers, who made ale from an herbal mixture called gruit, and as monks are synonymous with beer brewing in the Western world, it is still commonly found growing near old monasteries and abbey ruins.

PIPE VINE
ARISTOLOCHIA MACROPHYLLA

Pipe vine is an unusual flowering climber that can be found in shady woodlands and mountain slopes across eastern North America. It is a fast-growing, woody vine with large, heart-shaped green leaves that can measure 6 to 10 inches across.

In summer it produces yellow-green, lobed flowers that are 2 inches long and blushed with burgundy.

It is the shape of these flowers that gifts the vine with its name, as they resemble old European tobacco pipes. It is also known as Dutchman's-pipe, and just like its smoky namesakes, the plant contains carcinogenic toxins.

Not a fan, huh?

The flowers also resemble little saxophones, but perhaps smooth, mellow tunes just weren't as popular as smoking back in the day.

Pipe vine's flowers can be tricky to locate, often hidden by dense layers of foliage, but their heady fragrance attracts pollinators, so follow the flies to find them. The funnel-shaped blooms can actually trap pollinators, as their entrance is lined with fine hairs that point inward, making exiting difficult. However, the plant is not carnivorous. Amazingly, it secretes sufficient dewy nectar to keep the captive insect alive long enough to ensure pollination occurs—then the flower opens again, releasing its pollen-covered prisoner.

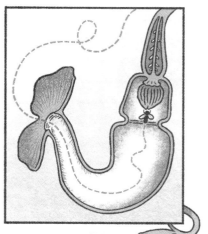

The flowers mature into seed-laden cucumber-like fruits in autumn.

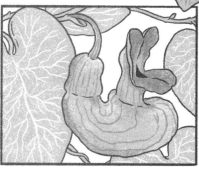

There are many wild and ornamental species of pipe vine growing around the world, including regional American species: California pipe vine (*A. californica*), which has similarly shaped but distinctively veined flowers, and Texas pipe vine (*A. reticulata*), with its tiny, fuzzy burgundy-and-white blooms.

BIRD'S-FOOT TREFOIL

LOTUS CORNICULATUS

This flowering legume is native to Eurasia and Africa but has naturalized around the world, where it can commonly be found in grasslands and roadside verges.

In summer, bird's-foot trefoil grows on simple branching stems tipped with bright green trios of leaflets. The flowers are yellow and pealike, often blushed with orange or red. The plant has a variable height, either low growing and trailing in open areas or up to a foot tall when supported by other plants in crowded meadows.

The bird's-foot name comes from the shape of its seedpods, which follow the flowers and develop into dark bunches of clawlike fingers.

For me?

In the Victorian language of flowers, bird's-foot trefoil symbolized revenge.

PEARLY EVERLASTING

ANAPHALIS MARGARITACEA

This dreamy wildflower is native to North America and Asia, where it can be found growing on gravelly roadsides, rocky mountain slopes, and open meadows across much of the continent. It has also naturalized in Europe.

Pearly everlasting has narrow, delicate leaves that are green on top, with silvery, woolly undersides, and grow alternately from erect stems that reach up to 3 feet high.

It begins to bloom in midsummer, producing clustered heads of tightly packed white buds, which are rounded and pearl-like. These open to reveal golden-yellow centers, tightly clasped by a multitude of tiny, scaly white petals. The flowers can have a light, musky aroma.

As their name suggests, the flowers endure well after their summery neighbors have given up. If cut, they are indeed everlasting and will retain their beauty in a posy vase, dried floral arrangement, or crafted wreath—a dainty, bright reminder of summer to enjoy in the darker months.

BRACKEN

PTERIDIUM AQUILINUM

Bracken is a bushy fern that grows in temperate regions around the world. Its tentative fronds unfurl in spring, and by summer you can find its broad leaves sprawling over woodlands, hills, and moors.

Bracken's triangular leaves fan out from sturdy, hairy stems, secured underground by thick rhizome roots. When mature, the foliage has a leathery, green upper surface and reaches 2 to 5 feet high.

Bracken uses spores rather than seeds to reproduce. These develop in tiny brown sacs tucked under the outer edges of its leaf fronds. The dusty spores are incredibly light and disperse in summer, floating away gently on warm breezes.

In ancient Europe, people thought this spore release coincided with the summer solstice and attached superstitions to these events. It was said that anyone who caught the spores on Midsummer night would gain the power of invisibility. Bracken actually releases its spores later in the season, and excessive exposure to them can be carcinogenic.

It ain't worth it, invisible pal!

By autumn, the foliage dies back, turning rusty brown before wilting down to ground level.

The *aquilinum* part of bracken's name means "eagle" in Latin, referencing the wing-shaped fronds. This likeness is also referenced by an alternate common name:

Eagle fern

FIREWEED

This stunning wildflower is native to the temperate Northern Hemisphere, where it flourishes in waste places, verges, and dry, open areas.

Fireweed grows on upright, reddish stems with long, pointed leaves arranged in a spiral. In summer, a tapered wand develops at the tip of the stem, budding and blooming with many small pink or purple flowers.

By the end of summer, pollinated flowers mature into long, burgundy seedpods that split open to release clumps of tiny brown seeds with silky hairs. These seeds spread quickly and germinate with great success, creating large colonies of plants within a short period of time.

Fireweed's common name is derived from its hardy roots and seeds that can tolerate high temperatures and dry soils, meaning it is often the first plant to appear on scorched earth and burned habitats.

In Britain during the Second World War it was seen growing in bomb craters, which earned it the nickname:

Bomb weed

The young stalks of fireweed are edible and can be cooked like asparagus. Older woody stems have a soft, pithy center that can be scraped out and used as a thickener in soups, stews, and jellies.

In eastern Europe, fireweed leaves are fermented and dried to make a very popular and fancy tea called:

Ivan chai

ИВАН ЧАЙ

WILD MARJORAM

ORIGANUM VULGARE

Wild marjoram is a flowering herb, native to Mediterranean Europe but widely naturalized around the world, where it flourishes on hedge banks, mountain slopes, and grassy meadows.

It grows from a bushy base of oval leaves that appear in opposite pairs and are covered in fine hairs. In summer, clusters of small white or pink flowers bloom at the tips of erect reddish stems, which reach 2 to 3 feet high.

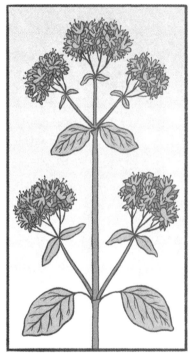

Wild marjoram leaves are edible and can be used, either fresh or dried, as an herb. This plant is also known as wild oregano.

Wild marjoram flowers have a sweet and spicy aroma. The ancient Greeks adored this fragrance so much, they believed that Aphrodite, the goddess of love, must have created it.

GREAT YELLOW POND LILY
NUPHAR POLYSEPALA

This swampy wildflower can be found in lakes, ponds, and slow-flowing streams across northern and western areas of North America. It produces glossy, heart-shaped leaves, which are waterproof and float, providing shelter for neighboring fish.

In summer, round flower heads rise from the water, blooming into bright yellow cups stuffed with radiating red-brown anthers. These blooms can reach 3 to 4 inches in diameter and mature into an oval, ribbed, green fruits that contain little seeds resembling corn kernels.

The seeds are edible and can be ground and cooked as porridge or baked into bread, or you can throw them into a hot pan to make a crunchy, popcorn-like snack.

The whole plant is anchored by submerged stems attached to a thick, sturdy rhizome. These roots have a history of use in folk medicine and have often been made into a gargling infusion to treat sore throats or chewed to relieve toothaches.

VIPER'S BUGLOSS

ECHIUM VULGARE

This wildflower is native to Europe and Asia but has naturalized across much of North America. It flourishes in dry, sandy soils on heathlands, cliffs, quarries, and wastelands.

First-year rosette

Viper's bugloss is bienneal, appearing in its first year as a rosette of rough, hairy, tongue-shaped leaves that are the origin of half its common name: from the Greek words *bous*, meaning "ox" or "cattle," and *glossa*, meaning "tongue." So we end up with *bugloss* . . .

. . . which is a mighty fancy way of saying "ox tongue."

In its second year it flowers and grows on thick, upright stems, which reach 1 to 3 feet high and are green with red spots. This coloration could be the origin of its name, as they also resemble the spotted patterning of a viper's scales, but other theories include the shape of the flower's pistil—which is forked like a snake's tongue—or the old medicinal use of the plant in treating snakebites. Whichever is true, it sounds intimidating and serves as a warning: do not touch! The whole plant is covered in fine, glass-like spines that prick and irritate the skin.

We'll bite ya!

This fierceness belies the colorful beauty of its blooms, which arrive in summer. They begin as red buds that turn into trumpet-shaped blue or lilac flowers with five distinct lobes and protruding purple anthers, tipped with blue-gray pollen. They are nectar-rich and attract all manner of hungry pollinators, including bees, butterflies, and moths.

This beautiful wildflower is native to North and South America, with a wide distribution, including many varieties and hybrids. It can be found growing in meadows, prairies, and mountain foothills and along roadsides and trails. It also appears in Europe and Australia, where it has become widely naturalized because of its hardiness and drought resistance, enabling it to thrive where other native plants cannot.

Blanketflowers grow from a spray of long, green leaves that gather at the base. Branching, erect stems grow up to 2 feet high, each tipped with a single flower. One plant can produce many blooms throughout summer and often into autumn.

Individual blooms can reach 2 to 3 inches in diameter and have a maroon center with radiating florets arranged in a beautiful, fringed disc. Flowers are often two toned, with red centers and yellow or orange tips.

This brightly patterned inflorescence is said to resemble the intricately woven textiles made by many Indigenous nations.

Blanketflower moth, Schinia masoni

The plant is a magnet for nectar-loving creatures, especially hummingbirds, butterflies, and moths. There are even moth species named after it, with fuzzy yellow heads and thoraxes alongside speckled maroon wings that perfectly camouflage on the flowers.

These moths depend on the blanketflower, laying their larvae in its seed head and using it as a food source. A beautiful insect's colorful dream home.

SOAPWORT
SAPONARIA OFFICINALIS

Soapwort is a hardy wildflower that was originally native to northern Europe. After being introduced by colonists and settlers, it is now seen throughout much of the Northern Hemisphere, where it can be invasive. It can be found in sunbathed fields, borders, roadsides, and stream edges.

Soapwort grows in spreading clumps, on unbranched stems that reach 2 or 3 feet high and bear blade-shaped, opposite leaves. In summer, its stems are topped with clusters of 1-inch, pale pink flowers, each having five petals and a light, clove-like scent.

As suggested by its common name, this wildflower has historic uses as a natural cleaning product. It contains chemicals called saponins, which produce a lather when combined with water, and the *Saponaria* part of its name comes from the Latin word *sapo*, meaning "soap." The cleaning agent was traditionally extracted by harvesting the leaves, stems, and roots and boiling them, which created a natural detergent to wash textiles. Crushing some leafy stalks and soaking them in water also makes a perfectly good emergency hand wash or foragers' shampoo.

YELLOW RATTLE
RHINANTHUS MINOR

Yellow rattle is a pretty summer wildflower that can be found in grassy fields, dunes, and meadows across the temperate Northern Hemisphere.

In summer, branching stems grow 8 to 12 inches tall, decorated with pairs of veiny, serrated leaves. Hollow yellow flowers bloom throughout the season, held in green saw-toothed cups.

Eventually the flowers fade and the seasonal heat dries them out, leaving delicate brown shells full of seeds that shake in the wind. These capsules create a rattling sound that lends the plant its common name. This sound often accompanies the late summer harvest, so the plant is also known as:

Hay rattle

COMMON CATTAIL

TYPHA LATIFOLIA

Common cattail can be found growing in dense, grassy mats near shallow fresh waters, flooded areas, and marshes. Its long, elegant leaves stand upright and unbranched in a decorative spray, and it has a wide native range across North and South America, Europe, Africa, and Asia.

In summer, flowering seed heads appear—green at first, then maturing into yellow and brown. The flowers can reach a foot in length and grow in two parts: a lower chocolate-brown, velvety poker, which is female, and a golden flower cluster, tapered at the top, which is male. These persist into autumn and winter, eventually bursting with downy seeds that stand on erect stems and look like sticks of cotton candy.

This plant's common name accurately describes its fuzzy wands, which peek through leafy reeds, suggesting a feline predator is stalking within.

You know, you're not the greatest conversationalist.

The fluffy seeds are water repellent and buoyant—so much so that they were used as replacement padding for life vests in the Second World War and emergency caulking to seal leaky boats.

Common cattail is also a natural bioremediator—meaning it readily absorbs pollutants from surrounding water and soil—and can therefore be planted in contaminated habitats, helping to restore them.

T. angustifolia

The closely related species *T. angustifolia* is also common in America and Europe. It is a thinner plant with tan-colored seed heads, understandably called narrowleaf cattail.

DEVIL'S-FIG

ARGEMONE MEXICANA

This wildflower can be found in South America and southern areas of North America. It is extremely hardy and drought tolerant, which means it often appears in waste areas, disturbed soils, and roadside verges. This advantage has enabled it to naturalize across much of the world, and in many places it is considered a weed.

Devil's-fig grows on stout stems of 2 to 3 feet and has waxy, prickly leaves, which are blue-green with white veins and pale edges. Both the stem and foliage weep a yellow sap when cut.

In summer, the vicious foliage frames a delicate, cup-shaped flower, with six yellow petals and a central red stigma. As these are similar in appearance to poppies, devil's-fig is often called prickly poppy or Mexican poppy. After pollination, the petals shed and the fruit matures into a pointed spine-covered oval.

This fruit resembles a fig, but it is said that its fierce armor thwarted any brave foragers who attempted to eat it, and so they would curse its supposed maker, dubbing it the devil's fig. If any did succeed and chew past the spines, they would also find that the seeds within are dangerously toxic.

Yes, yes, more spines!

Oh delightful, fill it with poison, too!

CHECKLIST

- ☐ Black walnut
- ☐ Hoof fungus
- ☐ American lotus
- ☐ White snakeroot
- ☐ Nettle-leaved bellflower
- ☐ Hobblebush
- ☐ Common bird's-nest
- ☐ Self-heal
- ☐ Ghost pipe
- ☐ Cardinal flower
- ☐ Groundnut
- ☐ Eastern white pine
- ☐ Bog moss
- ☐ Wild chicory
- ☐ Traveler's-joy
- ☐ Sassafras
- ☐ Dog rose
- ☐ Scarlet pimpernel
- ☐ Beefsteak fungus
- ☐ Blackthorn
- ☐ Shaggy ink cap
- ☐ European spindle

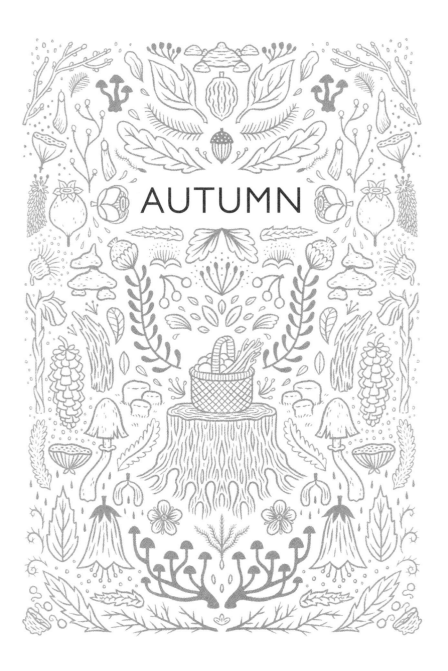

AUTUMN

BLACK WALNUT

JUGLANS NIGRA

This majestic tree can be found in forested areas, near water, and on hillsides across central and eastern parts of North America. It has also naturalized in Europe. When black walnut grows in the open, it can appear broad and spreading, with a branched trunk, but in more heavily wooded areas, it will have a straight trunk with few lower branches. It is fast growing and can reach 50 to 75 feet in height, sometimes more.

In spring, pale buds covered in silky hairs emerge on the branches and develop into hanging male catkins and upright female flower clusters. By summer, the tree is in full leaf, covered in long, arching stems fringed with tooth-edged leaflets. Both the foliage and bark have a distinctively pungent, spicy smell.

In autumn, the whole tree turns golden yellow and spherical green-brown fruits mature. These eventually turn black and drop off in October, releasing small, corrugated black nuts.

These nuts are edible, but if you find any, be warned that the shell is extremely hard, making kernel extraction challenging. Some foragers use rocks or even roll the nuts underfoot to release the tasty treats within. The shells are so tough, in fact, they are used in industrial sand-blasting mixtures and as abrasive cleaners. The *Juglans* part of the plant's official classification refers to its ancient name, *Jovis glans*, meaning the "nuts of Jupiter." A tough nut, all right!

Most parts of this tree contain natural dyes that can stain your hands and clothes. Colors range from a golden brown derived from the fruits to an inky, black-brown found in the husks and bark. These pigments can be used to make wood stain, textile dye, drawing inks, and a natural hair colorant.

Black walnut has a beautiful, rich brown heartwood, which is durable and highly prized—so much so that some trees have been known to be stolen by illicit gangs of walnut rustlers.

HOOF FUNGUS

FOMES FOMENTARIUS

This tough, woody fungus can be found on broken bark and fallen trees throughout Africa, Asia, Europe, and North America. It grows all year round but is easiest to find in autumn and winter when foliage is sparse and decaying wood is plentiful. It grows in a rounded bracket measuring 4 to 12 inches across, marked with horizontal stripes in varying shades of brown and gray.

The underside of this fungus is flat and finely pitted with pores, and—as its common name suggests—its overall shape is that of a horse's hoof.

Another common name is tinder fungus, which reveals one of its many uses: lighting fires. The fungus has dense, cinnamon-colored interior flesh that can be cut, dried, and shredded to create a starting fuel that readily combusts and creates long-lasting embers. This is also reflected in its Latin name, derived from *fomentum*, meaning "kindling."

A piece of hoof fungus was found among the possessions of Ötzi the Iceman, an ancient, mummified human discovered in the Alps. He was extremely well preserved in a glacier, where archaeologists found that he also carried pieces of flint and pyrite, suggesting that this fungus has been known to and used by humans to start fires for more than five millennia.

The fibrous body of hoof fungus can be boiled, soaked, and pounded flat to make a traditional fiber called amadou, a felty, suede-like fabric used to make convenient kindling strips, as well as hats, clothing, and absorbent wound dressings.

Some modern sustainable fashion brands have begun replacing animal leather with plastic-free mushroom fiber alternatives.

AMERICAN LOTUS
NELUMBO LUTEA

This flowering aquatic plant is native to eastern and central parts of North America, Mexico, and the Caribbean, but it also grows in Asia. In spring and summer, it can be found around marshes, lakes, and shorelines. Its huge, circular leaves with radiating veins are suspended on and above the surface of water, each held by a central stem. Blue-green in color, these magnificent leaves can reach diameters of 1 to 3 feet—the upper leaves becoming bowl shaped to create rain-water-catching basins.

Over summer, the lotus produces light yellow flowers that rise from the water on naked stems and measure 8 to 10 inches across—these are one of the largest native flowers in the United States. They are spectacular and sweetly fragrant but last only a few days before shedding their petals to leave a bare, orange-yellow central receptacle.

In autumn, the flowers' cone-shaped centers mature into wonderfully iconic showerhead-shaped seedpods. They turn from yellow to green, eventually becoming dark brown, hardened, and pitted with holes. Each hole contains a seed that can be shelled and eaten like a peanut or harvested later in the season and ground to make a sweet, chestnutty paste.

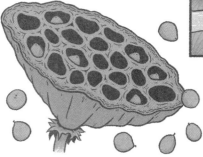

This is reflected in another of its common names, water chinquapin, which uses the Algonquian word for "chestnut," *chinquapin*.

Most of this plant is edible, and many Indigenous nations distributed it across the continent as a valuable food source, which it provides all year round. In spring and summer the young, unopened leaves can be used like spinach, while autumn brings the peanut-like seeds and winter yields the starchy roots, which can be roasted like a sweet potato.

WHITE SNAKEROOT

AGERATINA ALTISSIMA

This wild herb can be found in woodlands, thickets, and borders across central and eastern parts of North America, growing 3 or more feet tall on smooth, upright stems with pointed, toothy leaves. It blooms in autumn, producing frothy clusters of small white flowers. In winter, a fluffy crown of seeds is dispersed on the wind, settling in cracks and exposed soil, ready to appear again the following autumn.

This herb's common name comes from an erroneous folk medicine remedy that used the rhizome to treat snakebites.

Despite containing a poisonous toxin called tremetol, white snakeroot is often grazed upon by wildlife, including dairy cows. The milk produced by these animals continues to be poisonous when drunk by humans, which sadly led to many unexplained deaths in settler communities, including that of Abraham Lincoln's mother, Nancy. The mysterious "milk sickness" persisted until the early twentieth century, when research papers revealing its cause were finally circulated. A pink variety, *A. occidentalis*, which is common in the western United States, does not have these toxic effects.

NETTLE-LEAVED BELLFLOWER

CAMPANULA TRACHELIUM

This beautiful wildflower is native to Denmark and the United Kingdom but has naturalized throughout Europe, Africa, and eastern parts of North America, where it can be found in shady woodland margins, hedges, and scrublands. The plant grows 2 to 3 feet tall on upright stems with bristly, toothed leaves, which, like its name suggests, look similar to nettle.

From summer to autumn it produces inch-long blue, purple, or lilac flowers with fuzzy insides that dip and nod in the breeze.

The *trachelium* part of its scientific name refers to an old folk medicine use for curing sore throats.

Another common name describes the shape of the flowers, with long stamens nestled in the downturned tubular blossoms: bats in the belfry.

Can I help you?!

HOBBLEBUSH

VIBURNUM LANTANOIDES

This shrub grows 6 to 12 feet tall in tangled thickets near streams, swamps, and moist woodlands throughout northern and eastern North America.

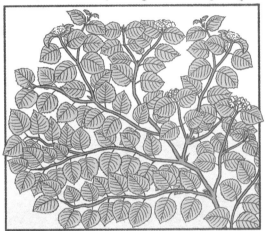

Hobblebush is a beautiful plant in all seasons. Winter provides copper-colored buds, followed by lacy white flower clusters in spring, and summer brings a verdant flush of heart-shaped, deeply veined leaves that reach 6 to 8 inches across.

Hobblebush is perhaps at its most magnificent in autumn, when its changing leaves display a palette of yellow, pink, red, and purple. Alongside the leaves are small berries, which first appear green, then red, ripening eventually to purple-black.

The plant gets its common name from the drooping outer branches that arch to the ground and take root. This creates camouflaged hazards that catch the feet of passersby and trip them, causing them to "hobble" home. Nature's leafy prankster.

The velvety buds and twigs are a precious late-year food source for browsing deer. The berries are eaten by squirrels, chipmunks, and songbirds, and are nontoxic to humans, with a flavor much like prunes or dates.

A snacky peace offering for causing all those stumbles.

COMMON BIRD'S-NEST

CRUCIBULUM LAEVE

This tiny fungus grows from spring to autumn across most temperate regions of the Northern Hemisphere. It appears singly or in small clustered groups on decaying bark, fallen twigs, and plant mulch, so it is most commonly seen in autumn when an abundance of these litter the ground.

The young fungus is a short cylinder with a yellow- or orange-covered top and velvety sides. As it matures, the top ruptures to reveal a cup-shaped interior containing round, white spore packets called peridioles—an arrangement resembling a miniature bird's nest filled with eggs. The fungus is very small and inconspicuous, measuring only 1/8 inch in diameter, and may require some extra effort and attention to find.

It has a very descriptive scientific name. *Crucibulum* comes from the medieval Latin word for a "bowl-shaped melting pot," used in metallurgy, which mimics the shape of the mature fungus cup. *Laeve* derives from a Latin word for "smooth" and describes the fungus' inner surface.

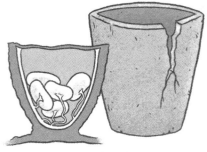

The egg-filled cups rely on rainfall for dispersal. When droplets land inside the cup, the spore-filled peridioles are flung out of their cozy nest.

Each "egg" is attached to the main fungus by a tiny cord, which snaps when they are ejected and wraps around nearby surfaces, attaching onto them and hatching anew. Some spore packets wrap around blades of grass, which are then eaten by grazing animals and dispersed even farther afield.

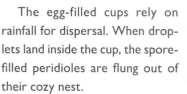

I'm hitching a ride outta here!

A small, herbaceous plant that can be found growing in roadside verges, woodland clearings, wastelands, and lawns, self-heal has a large native region in the Northern Hemisphere but has naturalized in most temperate areas of the world.

Self-heal appears in low-growing, matted patches, around a foot in height. Its leaves are varied in size, either oval shaped or pointed, and its flowering stems are square, hairy, and sometimes blushed with red. Club-like clusters of flowers appear from summer and last well into autumn. The individual flowers are violet and hooded with a three-lobed lower lip.

In late autumn, after the flowers fade, a maroon-brown seed head develops and remains on the stem until winter.

The whole plant has a long history of use in folk medicine as a treatment for wounds, bruises, throat infections, fevers, and cold sores, to name but a few. Other common names such as heal-all and woundwort reflect its reputation as a miracle plant.

Self-heal was also commonly used as a potherb, its leaves and stems added to soups and stews or eaten raw in salads. These many historic uses meant it was a well-traveled and -traded plant, which is why it now appears so widely around the world.

GHOST PIPE
MONOTROPA UNIFLORA

This unusual plant can be found on shaded woodland floors from summer through autumn in temperate regions of North America, South America, and Asia.

Ghost pipe grows 3 to 9 inches high on upright, pallid stems tipped with a bell-shaped flower that droops as it matures. Both the stems and flowers have glassy, translucent scales that are incredibly delicate and melt away when bruised.

This plant is white, or sometimes pinkish, and remarkably bears no green parts, as it doesn't contain chlorophyll or photosynthesize for energy. Instead, ghost pipes tap their roots into existing fungi networks attached to trees, parasitically siphoning off their nutrients.

They are most likely to appear in autumn after rain when the forest floor is covered in decaying debris and the fungi networks upon which they depend are most abundant.

An ethereal freeloader.

Ohhhhh nooooo, I forgot my wallet again!

CARDINAL FLOWER

LOBELIA CARDINALIS

This wildflower can be found across much of North America, from eastern Canada to the southwestern United States and into South America. Preferring moist soil, cardinal flowers often grow near water and swamps and in wooded areas.

The plant grows in clumps from a base rosette of glossy, lance-shaped leaves, with ridged, upright flowering stalks that reach 3 to 4 feet high. In both summer and autumn, each stalk produces a dense spike of bright red flowers.

Glad we all got the dress code memo.

This intense crimson coloring is reminiscent of robes worn by Catholic cardinals, who lend the flower its name. Interestingly, it is primarily pollinated by ruby-throated hummingbirds.

GROUNDNUT

APIOS AMERICANA

This herbaceous climbing vine grows in thickets and along riverbanks, where it scrambles over shrubs and trees throughout much of eastern and central North America.

Groundnut has slender stems that twine around nearby structures, reaching heights of up to 10 feet. Lance-shaped, vivid green leaflets grow from the main stem in groups of five or seven. In summer, pealike flowers appear in blushed pink, mauve, or maroon and have a sweet perfume.

In autumn, the vines produce green pods that contain edible peas. The rhizomatous roots can also be harvested at this time and look like a buried rosary, with stringy trails punctuated by round tubers.

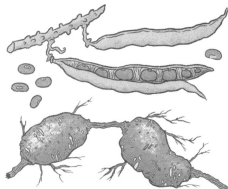

The roots can be prepared and cooked as you would potatoes, though they have a nuttier flavor and contain three times as much protein as their tuberous siblings. In winter, the whole plant dies back and becomes dormant until the following spring.

Groundnut has been a staple food for many Indigenous nations. It is also known as potato bean and hopniss, the latter being derived from the Lenape word *hopënis*, meaning "potato."

Oh, groundnut! You're spoiling me!

In more recent times it has become popular with gardeners as a flowering ornamental. Whether you want pink petals, perfume, peas, protein, or potatoes, this bountiful plant provides them all!

EASTERN WHITE PINE

PINUS STROBUS

This tall evergreen pine provides color throughout autumn and winter. It is native to North America and can be found throughout eastern parts of the continent, growing in mixed forests, rocky highlands, or boggy, humid areas. The eastern white pine reaches over 100 feet tall, soaring high on a straight trunk with a crown of layered branches. It has been introduced to Europe and the United Kingdom, where it is also known as Weymouth pine.

Slender, blue-green needles are bunched on the branches in groups of five and reach 3 to 6 inches long.

The needles can be foraged to make a lemony, fennel-flavored tea. Older needles shed every few years in autumn and can be collected for weaving crafts, such as basketry and matting. They also make a great mulch for garden beds, keeping weeds at bay.

The tree's long, curved cones mature over summer and release winged seeds in September that are eaten by wildlife. Many bird species rely on this tree for cover, nesting, and food.

Convenient and cozy.

Eastern white pine is particularly common in the Adirondack Mountains. The name *Adirondack* comes from an Iroquoian word meaning "tree eater" and refers to the edible parts of eastern white pine trees, including the inner bark, which can be foraged as an emergency food.

BOG MOSS

SPHAGNUM PALUSTRE

This tufty, tangled moss grows all year round in marshy meadows, bog margins, and wet forests across Europe, North America, and Australia.

Bog mosses spread over the ground, clumping together to create large, matted carpets. These tousled tendrils are usually a pale green color but can fade to brown or dusty pink when deprived of moisture.

During hot summer months they can dry out completely, becoming golden beige and woody, waiting to be revived by autumn rains.

Bog moss has some amazing properties—it is able to absorb more than twenty times its own weight in liquid and is naturally sterile and antiseptic.

Sphagnum Dressings

These features made it incredibly useful to medical practitioners throughout history. In the First World War it was cultivated on an industrial scale by the Allies. When cotton bandages were scarce, they used this moss to dress the wounds of soldiers.

From the arctic tundra to ancient Europe and North America, roaming parents have gathered this moss as a natural diaper and absorbent bedding for their newborn babies.

Wild chicory can be found growing on roadsides and grasslands in its native Europe, North Africa, and Asia. It has also been introduced in North America and Australia, where it has naturalized.

This wildflower grows 2 to 5 feet tall from a base of toothy, lobed leaves supporting branching, upright stems that are stiff and hairy. It blooms in summer and autumn, producing short-lived, sky-blue flowers with radiating florets.

The young leaves are edible and can be enjoyed raw; however, they become bitter tasting while the plant is in bloom.

The long, fleshy taproot is also edible and nutritious. It can be foraged and cooked like a vegetable or roasted, ground, and brewed to make a caffeine-free coffee substitute. Because of this, it is also known as:

Coffeeweed

Traveler's-joy is a climbing shrub with grooved, branching stems and twining leaf stalks. It is native to the United Kingdom but is indeed a traveler, as it can be found throughout much of the Northern Hemisphere, where it grows along roadsides and in disturbed soils.

In late summer, traveler's-joy blooms with pretty, milky-white flowers that smell sweetly of vanilla and almond. As this plant often grows beside walking paths, the aroma became a pleasant companion for hikers and adventurers, resulting in its common name.

By autumn, traveler's-joy sheds its toothy, oval leaves, and its flowers transform into feathery seeds with long, fuzzy tendrils. These clump together into hairy mounds, which earn the plant another common name:

Old-man's beard

The fluffy seeds distribute themselves on the wind, settling on new soil and crevices, ready to be reborn and bring more joy next year. Birds will gather these seeds and use them to build extra-cozy nests.

SASSAFRAS ALBIDUM

Sassafras is an aromatic tree, reaching over 30 feet in height, and native to eastern and central North America, where it grows in woodlands and fields and along roadsides.

It blossoms in late spring, with small, yellow-green buds that mature into clusters of pale yellow flowers. Broad, glossy, green leaves follow the flowers and unusually appear in three shapes: oval, two lobed, and three lobed. The distinctive shape of these leaves has led to another common name, mitten tree.

Sassafras leaves have a spiced, fruity aroma when crushed and remain on the tree until autumn, when they show a spectacular color change through shades of gold, orange, red, and purple. Female trees also produce fruit in autumn—clusters of blue-black berries held on bright red stalks.

This tree has a fascinating history of controversial uses. In eighteenth- and nineteenth-century England, sassafras roots were used to make a thick, milky drink called saloop, which was a northern European variation of the orchid-based Ottoman and Roman salep. Saloop was first popularized as a healthy, sobering tonic but later became known as a cure for syphilis and gonorrhea, so drinking it in public became much less fashionable.

In North America, sassafras roots, leaves, and bark were used as a medicinal remedy and an ingredient in root beer and filé powder, a gumbo seasoning. However, in the 1960s, sassafras was banned, when studies found it contained a carcinogenic substance called safrole.

Today, this same safrole oil is used commercially to make perfumes and insecticides, but is also a precursor chemical in the production of illegal narcotics.

DOG ROSE

ROSA CANINA

Dog rose is a common species of wild rose native to Europe and found in hedgerows and waste places. It grows in scrambling thickets, from 3 to 9 feet tall, with toothy green leaves and thorny stems.

In summer it produces pale pink-and-white, five-petaled flowers with yellow centers. By autumn, the bush is laden with ripening red or orange fruits—also known as hips or rose hips—which are incredibly rich in vitamins and antioxidants.

The hips can be foraged, steeped in hot water, and strained to make an immune system–boosting tea, or used to flavor wines, syrups, and jams.

The *canina* part of its classification means "dog" in Latin and continues the pooch-related titles. These could be derogatory names, as dog rose flowers don't compare to the beautiful garden rose. Alternatively, they may refer to an old folk medicinal use; when someone had been bitten by a dog, the plant was used to protect against illness and rabies.

Modern uses of dog rose hips include a flavoring for a European soda called Cockta and the main ingredient in a traditional Swedish soup called *nyponsoppa*. The seeds within the hips are bristly and scratchy—a source of free itching powder for the mischievous.

The native dog rose in North America is *Rosa acicularis*, known as prickly rose, and is very similar to its European relative. It has equally edible hips but differs in that it has deep pink flowers and longer, straight thorns.

SCARLET PIMPERNEL

ANAGALLIS ARVENSIS

This weedy wildflower can be found growing on road-side verges and disturbed wastelands. Scarlet pimpernel's native range is Europe, western Asia, and North Africa, though it has naturalized near globally.

Scarlet pimpernel grows low to the ground on square, creeping stems with small, soft leaves that support taller flowering stalks. It is in bloom from summer to autumn with dainty red, purple, or blue flowers that measure ½ inch across and have pink and yellow centers.

The flowers are re-active to sunlight, open-ing their petals during bright spells and clos-ing up when dark rain-clouds roll in. This habit has lent it some interest-ing common names, such as shepherd's clock and poor man's barometer.

Well, what do you reckon?

FISTULINA HEPATICA

This visceral bracket fungus can be found growing on tree trunks—commonly oak and chestnut—across Europe, North America, and Africa.

Beefsteak fungus is also known as ox tongue and, as these fleshy names suggest, it has a meaty appearance. The young fungus is pink on top with a white underside; it looks like a cheeky, wet tongue sticking out between fissures of bark.

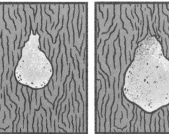
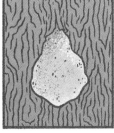

As it matures it becomes a wide, flat slab measuring 3 to 8 inches across and turns a deep red color, akin to a cut of tenderloin. The fungus even oozes red juices when its flesh squeezed or cut.

Total gore fest!

BLACKTHORN

PRUNUS SPINOSA

This shrub-like tree is native to Eurasia but was introduced to North America and New Zealand by settlers and has since naturalized. It grows in moist soil at the edges of woodlands, scrublands, or hedgerows, usually reaching 6 to 12 feet high.

In spring, blackthorn branches will flush with masses of white flowers, followed by small, oval, serrated-edge leaves that create a bushy foliage by summer.

In autumn its leaves turn yellow, and by winter a twisted black skeleton is all that remains. This plant gets its gnarly name from the dark bark and fiercely thorny spines of its branches.

After temperatures drop in autumn, you can find blue-black, plumlike fruits ripening on blackthorn's boughs. These measure ½ inch in diameter and have a chalky blush on their surface, which disappears when touched or wiped.

Blackthorn fruits, called sloeberries, are edible. They have an astringent taste when raw but become deeply fruity when cooked or preserved. They can be foraged to flavor gins and puddings, or used to make wines and jams.

The timber of blackthorn is twisted but tough, often used to make decorative tool handles and walking canes. The plant has a long association with ill omens and sorcery, as it was believed witches would use black-thorn branches to craft powerful wands and staffs known as black rods.

SHAGGY INK CAP

COPRINUS COMATUS

I n summer and autumn this curious fungus can be found growing in open grasslands and urban green spaces throughout Europe and North America.

The young mushroom has a pale white egg-shaped cap, blushed with brown toward the top. It grows 2 to 6 inches tall, and as it matures, its outer surface breaks up into scales that curl outward, giving it a shaggy appearance.

The mushroom is also known as lawyer's wigs, because at this stage they are visually reminiscent of the hairpieces traditionally worn by British judges and barristers.

Eventually the lower cap breaks away from the stem, exposing the gills, which turn black and liquify into an inky, dripping ooze.

The young mushrooms are edible but have a very short shelf life once picked. If you leave the foraged delights too long, they disintegrate into a puddle of black sludge.

If you cook older mushrooms that are already turning black, they will dye everything in your pot black, too.

Cool soup.

Thanks.

European spindle is a shrubby tree that grows 5 to 20 feet tall, depending on habitat and age. It is native to Europe and western Asia but widely naturalized elsewhere, including eastern parts of North America.

Spindle trees prefer chalky soils, growing in open forests and hedgerows. In spring and summer it has an understated appearance, with simple, finely toothed green leaves and clusters of small, greenish-white flowers.

In autumn the plant bursts with color as its foliage turns shades of yellow, red, orange, and purple. Bright-pink fruits ripen into hanging, four-lobed pods that split to reveal dazzling orange seeds that may persist into winter.

While the leaves and berries of this tree are poisonous to humans, its branches are smooth and splinter resistant, which made spindle twigs a favorable choice for skewers and toothpicks in the past. It gets its common name from another use—as spindles—which are long spikes used for spinning fibers and wool into thread.

Today, the dense wood is most commonly used to make high-quality artists' charcoal.

FIELD NOTES

FIELD NOTES

FIELD NOTES

FIELD NOTES

ABOUT THE AUTHOR

Kristyna Baczynski is an author, illustrator, and cartoonist who has been making comics, zines, and prints for fifteen years. Her debut graphic novel, *Retrograde Orbit*, was released in 2018, and her first author-illustrated children's book, *Read All About It*, followed in 2019.

Her Ukrainian grandparents, Anna and Mykhailo, and her aunt Darka inspired her love of nature. Their immense and practical knowledge of plants and wildlife seeded this book.

Kristyna lives in Leeds, UK, with her husband, cat, and small but wild garden.